KU-633-598

TANEY

PROGRESS OF A PARISH

Carol Robinson Tweed, B.A. (Mod.), M.A. (TCD), M.Sc. (UU), D.S.A., C.Q.S.W., M.B.P.S., M.A. (OU), was born in Belfast and attended six schools and three universities in Northern Ireland, England and the Irish Republic. She took Master's degrees in History and Political Science, Social Sciences and Post-Colonial English Literature, and professional qualifications in Social Work and Psychology.

Carol worked at a senior level in the Irish Probation Service and then ran her own psychology business. She was a board member of Irish Pen and on the Steering Committee of the UNESCO City of Literature scheme. She has written many articles for magazines and newspapers. Since retirement, Carol has served as President and Chairperson of a national charity.

Her first book, *Taney, Portrait of a Parish,* was published in 1994.

Carol is a Church Warden and is actively involved in Taney Parish. She lives happily in Dublin with Tom and close to her two adult children.

CAROL ROBINSON TWEED

TANEY

PROGRESS OF A PARISH

A SOCIAL AND HISTORICAL PROFILE OF THE PARISH OF TANEY IN DUBLIN

THE O'BRIEN PRESS
DUBLIN

First published 2018 by The O'Brien Press Ltd,
12 Terenure Road East, Rathgar,
Dublin 6, D06 HD27, Ireland
Tel: +353 1 4923333; Fax: +353 1 4922777
E-mail: books@obrien.ie
Website: www.obrien.ie
The O'Brien Press is a member of Publishing Ireland.

ISBN: 978-1-78849-013-9

10 9 8 7 6 5 4 3 2 1
23 22 21 20 19 18

Printed and bound in Poland by Białostockie Zakłady Graficzne S.A.
The paper in this book is produced using pulp from managed forests.

Photographs courtesy of Dr Susan Hood of the RCB Library, Mr Trevor Stafford, Mr Walter Newburn, Mr Ossie Baily, Mrs Daphne Scott, Mrs Vivian Hood, Mr Edwin Doyle and all those who earlier donated photographs to Taney Parish Archive.

TABLE OF CONTENTS

THIS
RISH CHURCH OF
ANEY
ATION DATES BACK
SEVENTH CENTURY
ANY RESTORATIONS
N AT LEAST TWICE
THE LAST 300 YEARS
760, AND AGAIN IN
1910.14.

FOREWORD

A few days after my appointment as Rector of Taney Parish was announced in July 2012, I received a book in the post. Entitled *Taney: Portrait of a Parish*, it came from the author, Carol Robinson Tweed. It was a lovely gesture, giving both myself and my wife Vera a useful and informative introduction to the Parish where I had been called to serve. The one disappointment was that it only covered the life of the Parish up until the early 1990s. So much has changed in the past twenty-five years – not just in Taney Parish, but in the world in which we serve and to which we minister. Within the wider Church of Ireland, we have embraced the ordination of women, the re-marriage of divorced persons in church and the publication of the 'new' Book of Common Prayer in 2004. Associated with this, we have witnessed the development of less formal and more contemporary acts and expressions of worship. In response to this, aspects of the recent refurbishment of Taney church provide for greater flexibility and more modern modes of communication.

In the wider society, we have seen a rapidly growing secularisation. Times of unprecedented wealth, as evidenced in the 'building boom', were followed by the very hurtful effects of the 'crash'. As will be seen in the pages of this book, Taney Parish was not immune from the effects of these years.

What better time to update our Parish history than when we celebrate the two-hundredth anniversary of the opening of Christ Church Taney for worship? I was particularly pleased when Carol Robinson Tweed agreed, at my prompting and the invitation of the Select Vestry, to revise and update her original work. This is important, not only because it keeps the record of the Parish's progress up to date, but also because it puts the present in the context of the past.

I believe it will be a useful point of reference for those entrusted with planning for the future in years to come.

Whether you are a long-standing parishioner or a newcomer, a friend of Taney Parish or a person interested in local history or sociology, I hope you will find this book interesting and informative.

I commend Carol's update and revision of her previous book, and thank her for undertaking it.

Enjoy!

Rev'd Canon Robert Warren, Rector of Taney Parish,
January 2018

PREFACE

The twenty-first of June 2018 marks the 200th anniversary of the dedication service in Christ Church Taney, now known colloquially in the neighbourhood as Taney church.

The origins of Taney Parish in fact date back to many centuries earlier and, in truth, Christ Church Taney was not formally consecrated until 10 June 1872, when all the debt accruing from its building was cleared. However, the arrival in 2018 of the bi-centenary of the inaugural service gives us an opportunity to celebrate the progress of this wonderful parish.

This book has been produced to mark this celebration. It is an update to my previous one, *Taney: Portrait of a Parish*, published in 1994. Like its predecessor, its intention is not to be an analytical, academic tome, but rather to offer a short, readable, popular and accurate narrative history, based on original sources, to enhance the knowledge of the general reader.

In my earlier book, I described how I had discovered some old Preachers' Books and Parish Registers hidden away at the back of the church. I told of how these had offered a charming glimpse into life in Taney around the turn of the last century. The revelation by the then rector, Canon William Desmond Sinnamon, that he held Vestry Minute Books dating back to 1791, and the subsequent exploration of a treasure trove of diocesan records held by the library of the Representative Church Body, sparked off the idea of the original book.

Since that first volume, much has happened within the Parish. New parishioners and their families have joined us, and some old friends are no longer with us. Huge progressive social changes during recent decades in Ireland have brought a great new variety in the make-up of Parish families. Such diversity gives the parish a healthy, open, outward-looking ethos, ensuring a promising future.

The tower of our Parish church looking very pretty in the snow.

The Parish Centre, opened on 21 November 1992, has provided a tremendous social facility both for parishioners and for residents of the wider community. It is booming with activity, and has a great buzz all through the week.

The installation of the St George's Bells in the church tower has given much pleasure to bell ringers and listeners alike, while a growing awareness of the needs of those with disabilities and of older people has led to the provision of a first-class sound system throughout the Parish buildings and a chairlift within the centre.

Excavations carried out in the graveyard of St Nahi's church in 2002 and 2004 led to the discovery of two ancient Rathdown slabs, and further excavations close by in 2007 confirmed that a church foundation had existed here for many centuries.

The economic recession of 2008 led to financial difficulties for the Parish, and the collapse of plans for the building of a parish nursing home and sheltered housing complex. Ultimately, this was a valuable learning experience.

Taney is still the largest Church of Ireland parish in the Republic of Ireland, with around 760 families. Many curates have come to Taney over the past twenty years to complete their training, before moving on to lead their own parishes. The former rector, Canon Desmond Sinnamon, retired in 2011, and our current rector, Canon Robert Warren, enthusiastically took over the reins in 2012.

The village of Dundrum in South Dublin has grown and changed enormously over the past two centuries. Swathes of middle-class suburban housing have grown up where once stood the large estates and townlands of the privileged and the abjectly humble cottages of the rural poor.

The past twenty years have seen development in Dundrum on a scale not experienced here before. We are fortunate in the bequeathing in 1993 of Airfield, in trust for the use of the people, by former parishioner Miss Naomi Overend. This has given us all the opportunity to explore the beautiful house, gardens and lands of what is now an urban farm open to the public. The installation of the Luas tram lines in 2004 has brought us within fifteen minutes' travelling time of St Stephen's Green in the city centre. The opening in 2005 of the Dundrum Town Centre, a vast 'cathedral' of consumerism to meet every need, brings shoppers and from all over the city and indeed the island, and has changed the popular perception of our village for ever.

Yet, for those of us who live here, Dundrum is still 'home': we meet people we know whenever we walk along the main street; we often socialise together; we feel we are part of a community.

The tower of Christ Church Taney dominates the skyline of Dundrum. Travelling along the Luas line, the public has also become aware of our smaller, older church, with its fascinating graveyard. Taney, though, is so much more than two fine old buildings and the worship that takes place in them.

A church is built primarily for the worship of God, but it is the people who grow and sustain a parish, who give a parish its unique ambience, who in essence make a parish. Our Parish is rich in memories, and has witnessed many centuries of dedication and contribution by those who have brought us to this point. History is not merely a record of the activities of the famous, and the history of a parish not primarily that of the efforts of its hardworking clergy. It is the story of human experience, of values, lifestyles and attitudes.

Taney is fortunate in having so complete a set of records. In the fire at the Public Records Office in 1922, the pre-1871 records of 1006 parishes were destroyed. Those of the remaining 637, including those of Taney, were in the custody of their parish clergy, thanks to a decision that incumbents who could guarantee safe storage were allowed to retain their registers. In 1998–99, the older Taney records were transferred to the RCB for conservation in a special air-conditioned chamber. They can be read there by researchers.

All the information included in this small volume, except for some necessarily speculative material in the introductory and 'Origins' chapters, is based on original sources from the past 225 years. I have endeavoured to give a true account of the administrative, economic and social changes that have occurred in Taney during this time.

This is an account of faith and hope, of financial difficulties for the Parish and the overcoming thereof; of the development of ideas; of social progress and the emergence of respect for all individuals regardless of their background or personal choices. It is a story of industry, enthusiasm and caring.

Among those whom I would like to thank are Tom, Jennifer & Conor, as well as Canon Robert Warren, for their interest and encouragement in this project, and also the many parishioners and friends who have offered information, documents and photographs. The practical assistance of Tara, Maeve and Jo has been invaluable.

I hope you will enjoy reading *Taney: Progress of a Parish* as much as I have enjoyed researching and writing it.

Thank you,

Carol, 2018

LInda and friends serving at the Christmas Bazaar.

CHAPTER 1

AN INTRODUCTION TO TANEY PARISH

TANEY, or TAWNEY, a parish, in the half-barony of RATHDOWN, County of DUBLIN, and province of LEINSTER, 3.5 miles from Dublin, on the road to Enniskerry, containing 4,020 inhabitants. It is beautifully situated on a sheltered declivity near the base of the Dublin and Wicklow mountains, and comprises 3,691 statute acres, as applotted under the Tithe Act. The land, which is of good quality, is principally in demesne; the surrounding scenery is richly diversified, and the parish thickly studded with handsome seats and pleasing villas, most of them commanding interesting views of the city and bay of Dublin and the adjacent country …

The living is a Rectory, in the Diocese of Dublin, forming part of the union of St. Peter's, and of the corps of the Archdeaconry of Dublin: the tithes amount to £415-7-8d, The church, to which the erection of which the Late Board of First Fruits granted a loan of £4,300, in 1818, is a spacious and handsome cruciform structure, in the later English style, with a square embattled tower. The interior was thoroughly renovated in 1835, for which purpose, the Ecclesiastical Commissioners granted £256. The old Church is still remaining; one portion of it is used for reading the Funeral Service, and another is appropriated to the Parochial School …

This is how Samuel Lewis described Taney Parish in his *Topographical Dictionary of Ireland*, published in 1837, less than twenty years after the building of Christ Church Taney to complement the old St Nahi's Church.

The new Parish church of Taney was built in a Dundrum very different from that with which we are familiar today. At that time, Dundrum was a country village of 680 inhabitants. Its clean air attracted recuperating invalids from Dublin, and its numerous herds of goats reputedly yielded milk of high quality. According to the 2011 census, the Dundrum part of the Rathdown electoral area, which comprises Churchtown, Dundrum, parts of Ballinteer and Clonskeagh, and corresponds well with the reach of Taney Parish, now houses a population of 37,743.

Dundrum village in 1837 contained a post office, a Roman Catholic chapel, schools, a dispensary, an iron foundry and a number of large houses and small cottages. Nearby Windy Harbour, as it was then known, was part of the Parish and contained a silk-throwing factory belonging to a Mr John Sweeney, employing about eighty people.

Elegant residences abounded. In the immediate neighbourhood, Lewis tells us, were 'Wickham', the seat of W. Farran; 'Sweetmount', that of W. Nolan; 'Dundrum House', owned by J. Walsh; 'Churchtown', that of W. Corbet; 'Churchtown House', that of D. Lynch; 'Sweetmount Villas', that of James Burke, and 'Sweetmount House' owned by M. Ryan. Dundrum Castle, even then, consisted merely of one ruined tower.

Among those in the wider Parish area were 'Mount Merrion', the residence of a Mrs Verschoyle; 'Merville', that of R. Manders; 'Mount Anville', home of the Hon. Chas. Burton, second Justice of the Court of Queen's Bench; 'Taney Hill', that of W. Bourne; 'Bellefield', residence of T. Wallace; 'Drummartin Castle', of Mrs. Dawson; 'Moreen', of D. McKay; 'Anneville', of Sir George Whitford; 'Ludford Park', of G. Hatchell; 'Ballinteer Lodge', of Major W. St. Clair; 'Milltown', of Major Palmer; 'Eden Park', of L. Finn; 'Delbrook', home of E.G. Mason, and many more.

Some older parishioners today can remember many of these big old houses when they were still private residences, but for most the names are familiar only as the names of housing estates that have sprung up in the Parish since the 1950s.

Today, we can subscribe to the religious denomination of our choice, we have tremendous ethnic and religious diversity, and most residents of Dundrum live in comfortable circumstances. But two centuries ago, there was severe social and religious inequality.

The *Parliamentary Gazetteer of Ireland* of 1846 tells of a Dundrum where 'The cottages of the peasantry are of a very humble and rural character'. Indeed, the contrast between the incomes and lifestyles of those employed in menial capacities in the Parish and those of the wealthy people who ran Parish life in the nineteenth century was immense.

Moreover, the figure Lewis gives of 4,020 inhabitants of the Parish is somewhat deceptive, for while all residents contributed to Taney as required by the tithe system, that figure, noted in the *Parliamentary Gazetteer* in 1834, consisted of '1,059 Churchmen, 4 Protestant Dissenters, and 2,957 Roman Catholics'. The system of tithe collection was by now being challenged, however. The Catholic Emancipation Act was passed in 1829; the Irish Church Temporalities Act of 1833 made drastic changes in the structure of the Church; and discussions were beginning on disestablishment. The Irish Church Act of 1869 dissolved the union between the Irish and English churches, and the established church in Ireland became the Church of Ireland, independently responsible for its own administration and finances.

The effects of these changes will become evident in later chapters, but clearly it can be seen that St Nahi's and Christ Church Taney have, during the past two-and-a-quarter centuries, witnessed fascinating developments in the social, educational, economic and administrative lives of the Parish and its parishioners.

The modern Taney Parish is flourishing, constantly welcoming new members and experimenting with innovative forms of worship and fellowship. We are hugely optimistic about its future.

CHAPTER 2

ORIGINS OF THE PARISH

Taney Parish is the largest, and probably one of the most successful and buoyant, of the Church of Ireland parishes in the Republic of Ireland. Yet, while there has been much speculation by both academic and local historians, we have until recently had little hard evidence on its origins.

The ninth of August has been designated St Nahi's Day and, from time to time, the Parish has celebrated this date in its worship. Frankly, little is known for certain about St Nathy, St Nathi or, as he is better known nowadays, St Nahi. He does not merit a mention in the *Oxford Dictionary of Saints*. Butler, however, in his eighteenth-century *Lives of the Saints*, describes him thus:

> *St. Nathy Cruimthir, that is, 'the priest', was a native of the Luighne district in Sligo and is mentioned in the life of St Attracta, who was probably his contemporary. He is said to have been put to Achonry by St Finnian of Clonard, though the name by which he was known makes it unlikely that he was a bishop … No biography either in Latin or in Irish seems to be available.*

St Nahi is credited with having been the first to set up a centre for monastic life, possibly during the seventh century, on the site of the old St Nahi's church in Dundrum. Indeed, one explanation of the derivation of the name 'Taney' suggests that it comes from the Irish 'Teach Nahi', or 'Nahi's house', although another likely source is 'Tamhnach', meaning 'a green field, an arable spot'.

While tradition suggests that St Nahi was born around 529 AD, it has also been posited that he died in 610. We have no definitive proof of when he lived, but he is considered to have been a priest or bishop in the late sixth or early seventh century.

The connection of the name Nathi with Achonry in County Sligo is strong. In the Anglican Diocese of Tuam, Killala and Achonry is an Anglican Cathedral called St Crumnathy's, and in the Roman Catholic Diocese of Achonry there is a St Nathy's Cathedral and a St Nathy's College.

There is also a possibility of a connection with Tobernea Holy Well in Seapoint, near Blackrock in County Dublin, the name of which is thought originally to have been 'Tober Nathi', translated as 'Well of Nathi'.

In recent years, however, archaeology has begun to offer answers to us. Archaeological finds (of which more in Chapter 3, on St Nahi's church) in 2002, 2004 and on an adjacent site in the former grounds of Notre Dame School in 2007 indicate that there was a monastic site here between about 600 AD and 1000 AD. The two Rathdown slabs found in the graveyard indicate the likelihood that Vikings had settled in the area and had become integrated into the local community.

Moreover, the 2007 excavations have revealed two curving enclosures dating from the early medieval period. These appear to form to an outer boundary likely to have surrounded an inner enclosure around St Nahi's church and graveyard. These may have been built for defensive purposes, probably in the eighth or ninth century (Ref: Edmond O'Donovan), and there may once have been houses between the two boundaries.

Among the artefacts found by the archaeologists was a spur from the fourteenth or fifteenth century and various pieces of medieval pottery, including much of a Flemish red-ware jug. There was also an iron belt buckle from the sixteenth or seventeenth century, parts of a bucket and several leather shoe soles. This suggests that there had probably been a farm here. Although researchers were unable to deduce whether there was any certain connection between the farmers and Taney church, it seems likely that the church served to some extent as an administrative centre for the district.

At any rate, there seems little doubt that religious worship was taking place here for some considerable time prior to the Anglo-Norman conquest of 1172. By the mid-twelfth century, it is known to have been a rural see, which subsequently became the rural Deanery of Taney. By the thirteenth century, it embraced parishes as far afield as Coolock, Clonsilla, Dunsink, Coolmine, Cloghran, Chapelizod and Ballyfermot.

After the conquest, Taney church and its surrounding lands were assigned to the See of Dublin and, shortly afterwards, Taney became a prebend of St Patrick's cathedral (meaning that a stipend was assigned by the cathedral to the Canon of the cathedral who had been assigned to Taney).

The two Rathdown slabs, thought to be from the Viking era, excavated in the graveyard at St Nahi's. The first features a saltire cross, and the second a circular pattern.

In the mid-thirteenth century, Archbishop Luke granted both the church and the prebend to the Archdeacon of Dublin, in whose possession it remained until 1851, being served by curates appointed by him. In that year, the Parish was severed from the Archdeaconry, and henceforth rectors were appointed, the first being the Reverend Andrew Noble Bredin (1851–57), and the ninth the present rector, Reverend Robert Warren (2012 to the present date).

Two surveys of the Half-Barony of Rathdown were made in the mid-seventeenth century, both useful in ascertaining the geographical extent of the Parish at that time. That carried out by Charles Fleetwood, Lord Deputy, in 1654 describes the Parish of Taney as containing the townlands of 'Bellawley', 'Dundrum', 'Balintry' (Ballinteer), 'Rabuck' (Roebuck), Owenstown, Kilmacud, 'a moiety of Churchtown', 'Churchtown alias Tanee' and 'Tipperstown' (Tubberstown, the townland on which Stillorgan station was later to stand). The Parish is stated to be bounded on the west by Rathfarnham, on the south by the Parish of Kilgobbin, on the east and north by the Parish of 'Donnebrook'. The townland of 'Churchtown alias Tanee' is returned as the property of John Kemp, of the City of Dublin. Kemp, a tailor, held it under lease from the Bishop of Dublin; it contained eighty-eight acres, and the tithes belonged to the College of Dublin.

The Down Survey, carried out by Sir William Petty in 1657, gives the boundaries of the Parish as follows: on the north, the Parish of 'Donibroook'; on the east the parishes of Monkstown, Tully and Kill; on the south, the Parish of Whitechurch; and on the west, the baronies of Newcastle and Uppercross. The townlands included in the Parish were as follows: Dundrum, 'Ballintery', 'Rabuck', Owenstown, Kilmacud, Ballawley, 'Tyberstown', 'Moltanstown' and Milltown. This survey omitted mention of the 'moiety of Churchtown', and of 'Churchtown alias Tanee', but included that of Milltown: both were stated in the respective surveys to have been owned by

Sir William Ussher, and it is likely that they referred to the same townland. The owners of the townlands were listed by Petty as follows:

NAMES OF OWNERS	LANDS	ACRES
Colonel Oliver Fitzwilliam	Dundrum and Ballintery	562
Lord of Trimlestowne	Rabuck	500
Lord of Meryyoung	Owenstowne	100
Morris Archbold	Kilmacud	150
James Walsh	Ballowley	440
Deane of Christ Church	Tyberstowne	87
The same	Moltanstowne	294
Sir William Ussher	Milltowne	[no acreage given]
	Total acres:	2133

The church land is returned at 381 acres.

The earliest original records still belonging to Taney Parish are the Vestry minute books, which date back to 1791. These are useful for determining the size of the Parish, because the system of collecting money for the Church at that time included the levying of tithes and the townland was used for administrative purposes as an enumeration unit. Thus, for example, the accounts for 1794 list the individual landholders, their acreages and contributions. They are summarised as follows:

TOWNLANDS	ACRES	£	S	S
Balally	481	7	0	3½
Roebuck	600	8	15	0
Owenstown	111	1	12	4½
Callary	50	0	14	7
Rathmines	91	1	6	6½
Farmbolie	141	2	1	1½
Churchtown	220	3	4	2
Dundrum	668	9	14	10
	2,362	34	8	11

By 1837, Lewis is referring to 3,691 acres and, indeed, as the Parish grew, the old church was proving too small. As early as 1809, discussions had begun on replacing the Parish church with a new and more spacious structure. Christ Church Taney was completed and opened for worship in 1818, though it was not fully consecrated until 1872. In 1859, services were begun in a room in Mount Merrion, and the Parish's third church, St Thomas's, was built there in 1874. It finally became the separate Parish of St Thomas and Mount Merrion in 1956. In 1867, a licence was also granted for the performance of Divine Service at what was then known as the 'Dundrum Lunatic Asylum', and Church of Ireland services are still held at the Central Mental Hospital, as required, by the Taney clergy to this day.

By the turn of the twentieth century, Taney Parish comprised the following townlands, totalling 4,569 acres: Balally, Ballinteer, Churchtown Lower, Churchtown Upper, Drummartin, Dundrum, Farranboley, Friarland, Kingstown, Mount Anville, Mountmerrion or Callary, Mountmerrion South, Rathmines Great, Rathmines Little, Roebuck, Ticknock and Trimlestown or Owenstown. The census returns for 1891 record a population of 4,669, and a total housing stock with the Parish of 856.

The Parish as it now stands in 2018 is bounded roughly by Milltown to the north, the M50 motorway to the south, Churchtown to the west and Goatstown to the east, and comprises around 760 families.

CHAPTER 3

ST NAHI'S CHURCH

St Nahi's church sits at the edge of a substantial graveyard just off Upper Churchtown Road, on the edge of Dundrum village, surrounded by a stone wall and entered by early-twentieth-century wrought-iron gates.

The completion of the striking William Dargan Bridge and opening of the Luas light rail system Green Line in June 2004 has offered

An atmospheric photograph of St Nahi's graveyard and church.

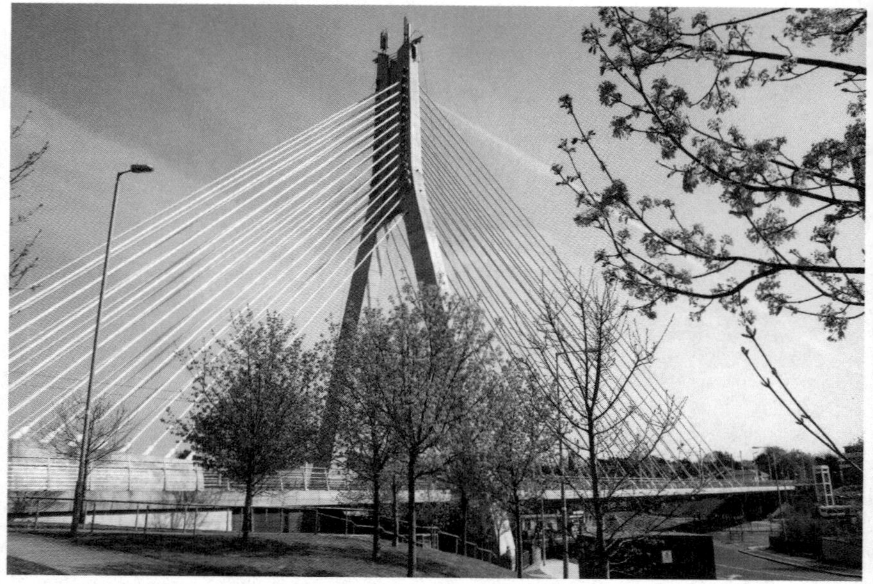

The futuristic-looking William Dargan Bridge, opened in 2004, which carries LUAS trams across the busy junction in the middle of Dundrum.

a splendid new view of the church and churchyard. Luas passengers can enjoy a particularly attractive impression of St Nahi's at night as, with the help of the Millennium Fund, floodlighting was installed around the church in May 2002, at a cost of €7000.

The present St Nahi's church building was erected in the middle of the eighteenth century as a result of the efforts of the then Archdeacon of Dublin, Dr Isaac Mann, and his curate, Reverend Jeremy Walsh. It was consecrated on 8 June 1760 by Richard Robinson, Bishop of Ferns and Leighlin, who later became Primate, and it had the distinction of being used the following year by the Bishop of Limerick for the ordination of priests.

It was designed in a simple rectangular box shape, and is mentioned in the 1846 *Parliamentary Gazetteer* as 'a small building of little interest'. Ball, too, thought little of its architecture, describing it in his *History of County Dublin, Part II,* as 'externally a singularly plain building, more resembling a barn than a church, and internally, the original reading desk and pulpit, (which still remain), rising above the Communion Table, show that it was equally devoid of ornament'.

Nowadays, however, we tend to regard its simplicity as part of its attraction and charm.

A visit to St Nahi's yields a number of points of interest. On the front wall is a plaque, reading as follows:

> *The entrance gate to this churchyard was erected by the Parishioners of Taney Parish to the memory of William Monk Gibbon, Canon of Christ Church Cathedral by whose inspiration and effort the restoration of this Church was accomplished. He repaired the Altar of the Lord.*

Externally, the church is simple and unassuming in style. The side walls are built of sandstone rubble, while the front door end (the west elevation) has a brick wall, rendered with cement-rich dashed mortar and a porch faced with dressed sandstone rubble. On top of this is a mock tower structure constructed of sandstone rubble. The church is roofed with dark grey slates, and the stained-glass windows are externally covered in mesh grids to protect them.

On entering the door to the front of the church, one is met with a small rectangular porch, with a decorative tiled floor and a sloping timber roof. To the right of the porch is the vestry, or robing room – a small room, almost square, with a low, flat, timber-sheeted ceiling. A small window is located on the south wall, with a coloured border, and the inscription 'I.H.S.' on the centre pane; on the west wall is a panel-doored cupboard. Also on the right-hand wall of this vestibule is a list of the church wardens who have served in St Nahi's over the years, culminating with Robert Lane and Elaine Wynne in 2015.

To the left of the porch, through small, wrought-iron gates and down three steps, is the baptistery. A plaque informs us that the gates were erected by the congregation in memory of Joseph Newman of Weston, Dundrum, who died on 24 May 1916. The floor of the baptistery is in decorative tiling, and the flat ceiling is of timber. The lower portion of the walls is decorated with stone panelling.

When the first edition of this book was published, the north wall had a plaque bearing the inscription 'To the glory of God and in memory of the men from this parish who fell in the war 1914–1918', but this has been temporarily removed while repairs to the wall are carried out.

The polished black stone baptismal font is believed to be that in which Arthur Wellesley – the first Duke of Wellington, acclaimed nineteenth-century military and political leader and victor at the Battle of Waterloo – was baptised in 1769. This font was transferred from St Kevin's church in Camden Row (by then a chapel of ease for St Peter's in Aungier Street), when St. Kevin's closed in 1912.

The window in the baptistery is by Evie Hone, and is her earliest. It depicts the Annunciation.

Importantly, displayed in the baptistry are the two Rathdown slabs, decorated grave slabs of a style found specifically in the area known historically as the Barony of Rathdown. One of these ancient stones was discovered in St Nahi's graveyard in March 2002 by Christiaan Corlett of Dúchas (as the Irish Heritage Service was known from 1995 to 2003), and the other was found in January 2004 by John Lennon of the Dundrum Historical Society.

Information given in the baptistery tells us that the former was protruding approximately twenty-two centimetres above ground level when first noticed, and it was moved to the church for safekeeping in March 2003. The latter piece is about seventy-one centimetres high, and is believed to be about one-third of the size of the original whole.

The baptismal font in the lobby of the church, flanked by the Rathdown slabs.

It seems that such stones were once thought to date from pre-Christian times, but are now considered to be from the Viking era and to reflect influences from Viking art. The first features a saltire cross, and the second has a circular pattern. The presence of these decorated stones offers evidence that human activity took place on this site at least one thousand years ago.

A pair of doors leads from the church porch into the nave.

To one's right, on the south side at the back of the church, sits the organ,

Top left: Marjorie Doyle, who played the harmonium in St Nahi's for many years.

Above: The old harmonium, as played by Marjorie.

Above right: The beautiful organ installed to mark the dawn of the new millenium.

and it is beside this that the St Nahi's choir sits during morning service. For many years, a small but ornately carved harmonium, made by D.W. Karn and Co. of Woodstock in Canada, was played at services, and this remains in the church. However, to celebrate the new millennium, a 1-manual tracker-action organ was installed. The Parish is honoured, at the time of writing this book, to have as its organist the internationally esteemed Dr David Adams, who plays at services both here in St Nahi's and in Christ Church Taney.

Looking eastwards, the nave is rectangular. The ceiling is timber sheeted and the centre aisle is laid out in decorative terracotta tiling on the floor, with woodblock herringbone-patterned flooring to each side. Two steps lead to the altar at the east end. The floor of the lower step is in woodblock to either side of a tiled centre portion. This is in terracotta tiles, in herringbone pattern, bordered in green, white and patterned cream and terracotta tiles. On this step are oak chairs, two prayer desks of carved oak and a lectern. The desks were

Light flooding in through the spectacular windows of St Nahi's, illuminating the 'barn-like' structure!

a gift from St. George's Church, Dublin, and are inscribed as being in memory of William V. Jolley and Gladys Wilkinson.

On the left-hand side is the pulpit. Formed from carved oak, it bears a brass strip inscribed 'The outer pulpit is erected as sacred to the memory of my beloved husband, William Barrington, of this parish, who died October the 14th 1900, and for the preservation of the inner eighteenth century pulpit'. The outer pulpit is in the form of open panels, with raised Maltese crosses at the top corners of the largest panels. The carved design on the cornice is in a Celtic interwoven pattern with leaf motifs at each angle. The inner pulpit is a single-panelled design with raised and fielded panels, painted black.

The book rest is in oak on an elegant brass bracket, which swivels. The altar rail on the next step is in a clover leaf cross-section in polished oak, hinged in its centre portion. It sits on four wrought-iron brackets. The altar is in oak, a simple table with three open panels to the front, each in the form of a painted arch, and a velvet curtain is draped inside the panels. Immediately above the altar is a picture of the Last Supper, bordered on each side by four tapestries. These are dedicated to Dr H. Montgomery, 1929, and Lieutenant E. Henry Montgomery, 1916; to the Rev Norman B. Harvey, Curate of Taney, 1929; to Florence Switzer, 1933; and to Mary Elinor Gibbon, 1917.

The four tapestries were created by Susan Mary Yeats (Lily, 1866–1949) and Elizabeth Corbett Yeats (Lolly, 1868–1940), sisters of the writer W.B. Yeats and the artist Jack Yeats. The Yeats sisters were high achievers in their own right. They were pioneers in Ireland of the Arts and Crafts movement, working in Evelyn Gleeson's Dun Emer Guild, a craft studio in Dundrum, from 1902. Lily was particularly talented at embroidery, and Lolly at printing. In 1908, they set up their own business, Cuala Press, in a bungalow in Churchtown. Cuala published over seventy books, including those of their brother W.B., Ezra Pound

IN
MEMORY
OF
THER AND SON
H. MONTGOMERY
T. E. HENRY MONTGOMERY

MEMORY
OF
THE REV. NORMAN B. HARVEY B.A.
CURATE OF TANEY
MUCH LOVED
1920

The four tapestries by the Yeats sisters, Elizabeth and Susan, which hang behind the altar.

The three windows at the top of the church, created by Catherine O'Brien (from left to right): 'The Miraculous Draft of Fishes', 'I am the Resurrection and the Life' and 'Disciples at Emmaus'.

and J.M. Synge. They lived in the family home, 'Gurteen Dhas' in Churchtown, attended St Nahi's church regularly, and are buried in the church yard.

On the window sill above the tapestries is a simple oak Celtic cross. At each end of the raised section are stands for prayer books.

A small brass notice is attached to the wooden panelling on the south side of the sanctuary, noting the retirement of Canon William Desmond Sinnamon and that altar frontals were presented by the parishioners.

The south wall windows are dedicated to Richard Irving Williams Barrington, who died in 1928, aged thirty-six; to Sarah, wife of Joseph Newman, of Weston, who died in 1915; and to Isabelle Agnes Gibbon, who died in 1945. Those on the north wall are dedicated to the memory of Henrietta Marie Jane Barrington, died 1933;

to Sophie J. Bond of Egremont, Cheshire, 1908 (produced by Meyer and Co., Munich); and to William Monk Gibbon, 1864–1935.

The stained-glass windows of St Nahi's Church are of particular interest, because most were the work of the well-known *An Túr Gloine* (The Tower of Glass) group of artists. This group, along with Harry Clarke, produced much highly esteemed stained-glass work in Ireland during the period from 1903 to 1963. The following artists produced windows for St Nahi's:

Alfred Ernest Child (1875–1939)
The Sermon on the Mount – 1929 (south wall)
Our Lord Walking on the Sea – 1934 (north wall)
Evie Hone (1894–1955)
The Annunciation – 1933–34 (baptistery)
Catherine O'Brien
I am the Resurrection and the Life – 1914 (east wall)
The Disciples at Emmaus – 1919 (east wall)
The Miraculous Draft of Fishes – 1919 (east wall)
After the Transfiguration – 1936 (north wall)
Christ Blessing Little Children – 1947 (south wall)
Ethel Rhind (1879–1952)
Praise the Lord – 1916 (south wall)

In addition to these *An Túr Gloine* works is a window on the north wall, known as the Caritas (Charity) window, made by Mayer & Co. of Munich and given in memory of Sophie J. Bond of Egremont, Cheshire, by her daughters in 1908.

Interestingly, this German-made window was found by a 2002 survey to be in perfect condition, though it was by then almost 100 years old. In fact, there are fifty-eight windows made by or attributed to Mayer & Co. extant in churches in the Dublin and Glendalough Diocese, attesting to their craftsmanship. Although

The beautiful windows of St Nahi's.

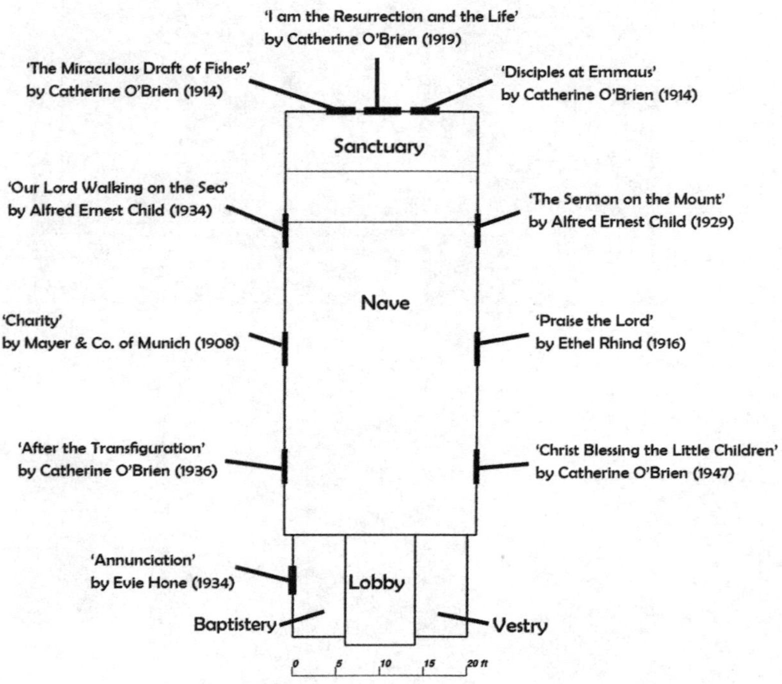

A floor plan of St Nahi's, showing the locations of the stained-glass windows.

they were long considered unfashionable, their quality and use of colour is now being reassessed.

A survey of the church by the United Diocese of Dublin and Glendalough on 16 April 2002 found some damage to the windows. It recommended the replacement of the old wire guards with new stainless steel ones, and some re-leading and repairs using modern techniques of conservation. In particular, the little Evie Hone window had been badly maintained, had been protected by unsightly wire guards and required restoration. This was subsequently carried out.

Commissioners for the Consecration of a Church
8 June 1760

Whereas the Minister, Church Wardens and Parishioners of Tawney in the Diocese of Dublin have erected and built a church in the said Parish, containing within the walls thereof in length from the East to the West, fifty feet or thereabouts, and in breadth from the North to the South, twenty two feet or thereabouts and have adorned and finished the same with all things decent and necessary for the service of God, and have humbly requested the Most Reverend Father in God Charles by divine Providence Lord Archbishop of Dublin Primate and Metropolitan of Ireland, that he by his ordinary and Episcopal authority, would be pleased to separate the said church from all Common and prophane uses and to consecrate and dedicate the same to holy and Godly uses. Wherefore, the said Most Reverend Father in God, willing to comply with their pious and religious intention but being so far prevented by various urgent affairs, and not to be able personally to perform the promises hath granted, and committed unto us his full power and authority in this behalf. We therefore, Richard by divine Permission Bishop of Ferns and Leighlin … do forever separate the said church from all common and prophane uses, and consecrate, devote and dedicate the same forever to the worship of God alone and the Celebration of Divine Service, and we grant, will and ordain that from henceforth, for evermore public prayers be openly read in the said Church according to the Holy Liturgy of the Church of Ireland, as by Law established, the Word of God sincerely propounded and preached, the Sacraments administered, and that all other matters be done and performed, which by the law of God and Canons and Constitutors of the laws of the Church of Ireland, can or may be done towards divine worship to the Glory of God, and the increase and prosperity of the church, and ordain, decree and declare that the said church shall and ought to be the Parish church, to and for the Parishioners, of the said parish of Tawney, forever and hereafter …

Dated the Eighth day of June in the year of our Lord
one thousand seven hundred and sixty

Of course, like any old church, St Nahi's requires frequent repair and improvement. In 2001, work on renovating the baptistery was started, and specialists were called in to renew the damp course.

In 2002, floodlighting was installed around the church at a cost of €7000, paid in part by the Parish, but also with the help of a grant of just under €2000 from the Millennium Fund. This highlights it in a very attractive way and is particularly striking when viewed from a passing Luas tram.

In early 2003, the Church benefitted from the provision of a polished brass Holy Communion rail, a gift by Brian and Val Kemp, in memory of Val's mother, Mrs McManus. This has proved very helpful for older and less abled parishioners.

The Select Vestry noted at this time that, as St Nahi's was a national monument, permission for alterations such as a fire escape would require planning permission and permission from the Heritage Department.

Over many decades, plans have been discussed to improve facilities at St. Nahi's by providing an extension to the vestry and toilets for the use of parishioners. However, apart from the difficulty of obtaining permission to add an extension to an eighteenth-century building, such plans have been thwarted by a lack of access to mains water and sewage, and to date, these improvements have not been carried out. In September 2002, the Select Vestry was again seriously investigating the possibility of adding a water supply and septic tank, but were unable to advance their plan. In January 2008, the Select Vestry had plans drawn up for an extension to the vestry room and for toilets, an extended baptistery and an exhibition area. Written comments were invited from St Nahi's attendees. At this stage also, water was coming through the roof. Further investigations were carried out in 2010, and are continuing. At present, negotiations are ongoing with Dun Laoghaire–Rathdown County Council, and it is hoped that the issue will be resolved before long.

In 2008, from 19 to 21 September, a popular festival was held in St Nahi's church to celebrate the stained-glass windows and historical artefacts. Called 'Lighten Our Darkness: The Stained Glass and Historic Artifacts in St Nahi's Church, Dundrum', it began on the Friday evening with a reception and the opening of an exhibition by Mary Hanafin TD, Minister for Social and Family Affairs. Admission was free. The occasion served to draw the attention of many people from the wider community, and was very successful.

Until 2011, there was no microphone in St Nahi's church, and many older parishioners found it difficult to hear readings and sermons. Following representations by the writer of this book, an excellent sound system, including microphones and a loop system, was installed. This has made a significant difference to the worship experience of many.

Today, St Nahi's church and its graveyard sit on an island, surrounded by traffic-filled roads and the shiny elegant new cable-stayed William Dargan Bridge, carrying Luas passengers across the huge Dundrum junction. Yet St Nahi's provides a little oasis of calm amidst the frantic rush of modern life, a place of quiet and contemplation. It is a building over two-and-a-half centuries old, but a monument to over a millennium of worship on this spot. Every Sunday morning it is filled with parishioners, enjoying a quiet and peaceful service.

CHAPTER 4

THE GRAVEYARD AT ST NAHI'S CHURCH

St Nahi's church sits amidst a large and beautiful churchyard, which features in the earliest documentation available about the Parish. It pre-dates the disestablishment, and graves of people of all Christian denominations can be found here. There are over 1,200 traditional graves, with perhaps three times that many bodies in them, and we can attribute names to around 900 of them. These names can be referred to in the modern index to the graveyard, held by the Parish.

An old postcard featuring St Nahi's church and 'Churchtown Cemetery'.

To describe the inscriptions on all the gravestones still in existence would be beyond the scope of this small book, but the curious reader may find the listings in *The Parish of Taney: A History of Dundrum, near Dublin, and its Neighbourhood* by Francis Elrington Ball and Everard Hamilton, published by Hodges Figgis and Co. Ltd. In 1895, helpful in this regard. Many of the gravestones described by Ball have since disappeared. He describes, for example, two seventeenth-century headstones, but present-day searches reveal none remaining from the seventeenth century,There are twelve extant headstones from the eighteenth century, and the vast majority of the remainder are from the nineteenth and twentieth centuries. Some graves, however, are older than they appear. Many twentieth-century bodies have been buried in existing graves, and in some cases, new gravestones have been erected to replace older ones that had been damaged or had disappeared.

A stroll around the graveyard provides a fascinating glimpse into the past of Taney Parish, and of Irish society in general.

A noticeboard just inside the gate gives details of well-known people buried within the graveyard, and a podcast trail was developed in 2010 by parishioner Harry Griffith. Visitors can use this as a guide when exploring. Included are Elizabeth Corbett Yeats (Lolly) and Susan Mary Yeats (Lily), sisters of writer W.B. Yeats and artist Jack Yeats. As noted in Chapter 3, these two worked in Dun Emer Industries and developed the Cuala Press. Indeed, Lolly is credited with being the first woman in Ireland to run a private printing press. As mentioned previously, the sisters were St Nahi parishioners.

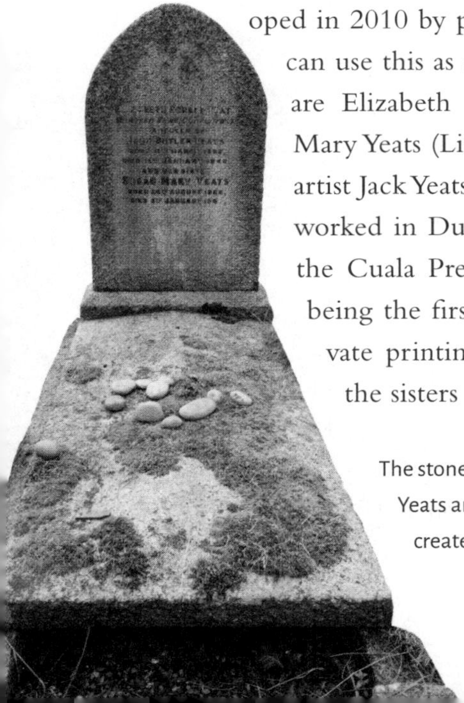

The stone marking the grave of the Elizabeth Corbett Yeats and Susan Mary Yeats, the sisters who created the beautiful tapestries in the church.

Other well-known people mentioned include:

- **Canon Monk Gibbon,** Rector of Taney from 1901 to 1935, and his writer son, William Monk Gibbon.
- **Canon William Alfred Hamilton**, Rector of Taney from 1867 to 1895.
- **Francis Elrington Ball**, who wrote *A History of the County of Dublin*, published in 1903, and who, with Everard Hamilton, co-wrote a history of Taney Parish, *The Parish of Taney, a History of Dundrum, near Dublin, and its Neighbourhood*, in 1895.
- **George Johnstone Stoney**, a nineteenth-century physicist and Boyle Medal winner, who first introduced the concept and later the name of the electron as the 'fundamental unit quantity of electricity'. He lived on Stoney Road, which is named in his honour.
- **Dr Isaac William Usher** of Laurel Lodge, who was famously knocked down and killed by a motor car in Dundrum in February 1917, and who is commemorated by a monument on Dundrum Main Street.
- **Lorcan MacSuibhne** (Lawrence Sweeney), killed during the Irish Civil War on 5 July 1922. A large crowd, including Eamonn De Valera, attended a ceremony in 1925 to unveil a memorial to him.
- **Patrick Doyle**, son of the above, who was killed in the Civil War at Crooksling, County Dublin.
- **James Burke**, one of the spectators shot dead at a Gaelic football match in Croke Park on 'Bloody Sunday', 21 November 1920.
- **Seamus Brennan**, former Fianna Fail TD and government minister, who died on 9 July 2008.

The graves of the less well-known too often catch one's attention – the names of families, both Protestant and Roman Catholic, whose descendants we know and meet around the village.

Perhaps saddest of all are the inscriptions to children, a reflection of social conditions thankfully now gone. The old *Index to Register of Burials in the old Parish church graveyard – Taney Parish – January 2nd 1897 to April 28th 1917* gives a shocking insight into life expectancy at that time. During those twenty years, no less than 1,836 people were laid to rest in St Nahi's. Of these, 551 appear to have been children aged six or under – a horrific number given that it refers to a period so recent in memory. In 1897 alone, 128 people were buried in St Nahi's, of whom fifty-seven were children under fifteen and forty-seven were children aged six or under.

To the left of the entrance gate, at the northwest corner of the church, lies another haunting reminder of harsher times – the Central Mental Hospital plot. At its foundation in 1850 as the 'Central Lunatic Asylum Dundrum for the reception of Insane Persons', the hospital benefited from the appointment of the curate of Taney as Protestant chaplain, and St Nahi's began receiving patients for burial. The plot was consecrated on 5 December 1872, and the consecration document contains a sketch delineating separate sections as available for burials of Protestants and of Roman Catholics.

This communal grave, forty feet by fifteen feet, was to be the burial ground for patients until the mid-twentieth century, the last burials of patients apparently being those of William Goff on 15 July 1946 and Edward Duff on 26 November 1946 ('Register of Burials, 1923 to 1950'). For many of these patients, details such as their ages were not recorded in the burial registers as they were for other parishioners, as if they were somehow of less importance. One poignant and heart-rending entry reads 'May 11th, 1925 – a baby stillborn – Central Asylum'. No name is given, of baby or mother, no details at all. Nor were these unfortunate people afforded the dignity of headstones or individual markings on their graves.

From the early 1980s, the graveyard had been considered full, and only those with existing family plots were buried there. From the end of that decade, however, the unmarked graves of former hospital patients offered the people of Dundrum a further opportunity to choose to be buried within their own village. At a meeting of

A dramatic nighttime portrait of St Nahi's – the graveyard and church juxtaposed against the Luas bridge.

the Select Vestry in December 1989, it was suggested that part of St Nahi's graveyard could be assigned as a Garden of Remembrance for those who have been cremated. The idea was pursued and, the following November, the Eastern Health Board agreed to the use of the Central Mental Hospital plot for this purpose. During 1991, layout drawings were prepared and details finalised. It was agreed that the new plots should be shallower than the existing ones, so as not to disturb those already buried there, and that each plot should be allowed to be marked with a plaque or small stone. This work being completed, the ashes of a number of parishioners have been laid to rest in St Nahi's.

However, in 2017, following a long period of legal searches, a very small number of graves were found to be available, and were offered for sale at a commercial price to parishioners who had registered their names on a waiting list many years earlier. Nevertheless,

The Garden of Remembrance in St Nahi's graveyard, designed and built in part by offenders during their Community Service, where ashes of the deceased are interred.

little available space remains in the graveyard. Most of those buried in St Nahi's graveyard in the later twentieth and early twenty-first centuries have been cremated, their ashes being buried in the cremation plot. It is now becoming clear that more land will be needed for cremation burials.

Meanwhile, as far back as 1986, the Select Vestry, in response to the requests of parishioners, began to investigate possibilities of linking the church to local water supply and waste systems, but all of their efforts were thwarted. Discussions on the need for toilets at St Nahi's continued during succeeding decades.

As will be explained in Chapter 8 on the Glebelands, a quarter of an acre behind the library had been conveyed to the Rathdown Board of Assistance in 1945 for the building of a dispensary and child welfare clinic, but with certain covenants attached, as outlined. The RCB approved the release of the restrictive covenants to the

Dun Laoghaire–Rathdown County Council, on condition that the council connect the church to the nearby public water and sewage system. This would be of advantage to the County Council, as the clinic has long been closed and the land is now available for redevelopment.

In 2013, the Select Vestry agreed to the lifting of the covenants contained in the 1945 conveyance, on two conditions: that the Dun Laoghaire–Rathdown County Council returned the small piece of land adjacent to the road, which had been compulsorily purchased in 1945 for road widening, but not used; and that they agreed to connect water and sewage pipes from the roadway to the church for the building of toilets. The Vestry also asked them to erect the required toilet facilities, but the County Council refused this. On 20 September 2011, the RCB had approved the vesting of the small piece of roadside land as a possible location for a Columbarium, and this was subsequently recommended by the Diocesan Council. Negotiations are continuing between Taney and the County Council on these issues.

The Parish remains optimistic that these questions will be resolved soon, that the necessary bathroom facilities can finally be provided, and that the unused piece of land will be returned for Parish use.

The care and maintenance of the graveyard has appeared as a constant topic of discussion in Parish records over the past 200 years. Parish accounts for the year ending Easter 1795 include an entry detailing the payment of 1/5d to Thomas Reiley for 'Carriage of Graveyard Trees'. The year ending Easter 1800 saw the Curate, Reverend Matthew Campbell, reimbursed the sum of £1-4-9d for a new gate for the graveyard, while 10/= was spent on hinges for same, and 6/= paid for masonry work to the graveyard wall. Indeed, repairs to the wall crop up with monotonous regularity in the ensuing decades, as do almost annual purchases of locks and chains for the graveyard gate, suggesting that security was no less a problem then than now. By 1836, the graveyard wall was in such a poor condition that consideration was given to asking the church authorities for a grant to replace it, and two years later the wall on the east side was wholly rebuilt, that on the west side completed and a new gate erected. Yet, by 1854, it was being rebuilt once again.

The work of maintaining the graveyard itself was also an annual expense throughout the nineteenth century. In 1814, for example, 10/- was paid to T. Mooney for weeding the graveyard. Two years later, the rate for the same job was £1, and by 1843 it was £1-10-0d. In 1898, the Sexton, who was paid 5/- for each grave dug, was in trouble for not having dug a grave to sufficient depth, and in that year, £4-9-4d was spent on maintenance and mowing. A new map of the graveyard was commissioned in 1898, at a cost of six guineas, and was prepared by Mr F.G. Craig.

During the twentieth century, the graveyard was to benefit from the voluntary efforts of parishioners. At the Vestry Meeting of 15 April 1930, it was proposed that 'parishioners would be asked to lend a man occasionally for a day's work in the graveyard', but later, as social progress dictated that most people could no longer afford to keep staff, members of the Parish themselves became involved in giving their free time to the physical work of keeping the graveyard tidy. The Parish Priest of Holy Cross church, Father Perkins, undertook in 1967 to encourage his parishioners to help in this task, and later gave a donation towards the cost of upkeep.

The early 1980s saw volunteers working hard in the graveyard, but by now it was wildly overgrown. A Community Service scheme in the 1980s and a Fás scheme in the 1990s restored it to order and, since then, the work has been carried out by contracted companies.

In April 2000, the County Council served a Dangerous Structures Order in respect of the wall between the graveyard and the road, on the grounds of public safety and duty of care. Following two hearings at Dun Laoghaire Court, the Parish was required to secure the wall so that it would not pose a hazard to passing pedestrians or traffic. In consultation with the RCB, they complied.

While the graveyard continues to require continual maintenance and improvement, it is now in a very good state. It provides dignity for the deceased and is a very interesting place to visit. Many would say St Nahi's graveyard has rarely looked better in their lifetimes.

Chapter 5

Christ Church Taney

The publication of this book in 2018 is one of the events marking the two-hundredth anniversary of the opening of Christ Church Taney for worship.

Reverend William Monk Gibbon puts it in context for us in an article he wrote in the 1918 Parish Magazine, celebrating 100 years of worship in Christ Church Taney. The Reverend tells us that the church 'opened for Divine Service on Sunday, the 21st June 1818. The world was at war … in the year of the Battle of Corunna, 1809, it was suggested … to build at or near the old church and at a very modest cost: but in the year 1812 – the year of the Battle of Salamanca – it was decided to build on a new site, and in a much more ambitious way … at a cost four times the original sum proposed.' He continues: 'the foundation stone was laid in 1815, the year of the Battle of Waterloo, and in June, when the battle was fought'.

This article goes on to explain that the new church was built with some sacrifice from parishioners. He wrote, 'the parish was then but thinly populated, and many of the parishioners were poor, but they denied themselves, building in faith for future years, and thus for a century the fine tower of the parish church has stood out as a landmark above the wooded heights of the fairest portion of County

Our Parish church, Christ Church Taney, on Taney Road, Dundrum.

Dublin – a testimony to the religious faith and devotion of men (sic) who lived in stirring times and bore the burden of a bitter war'.

The extent of the wooded heights around Dublin may have diminished since 1918, but Christ Church Taney remains an important landmark in Dundrum, and the Christmas lights upon the tower each December serve to enhance this impact. Here is how it all began:

> *The modern church is a spacious fabric, surmounting elevated ground, serving as a landmark to mariners and commanding very fine views over the city, the bay and a lovely expanse of country, the numerous ornamental plantations of which combine, at this point of observation, into a massive richness. The edifice itself, however, is as artistically defective as it is pretending and substantial.*
>
> *The Parliamentary Gazetteer of Ireland*, Vol III N–Z, p.310 (1846)

The idea of a new, larger church was first mooted in 1809, but it was 1812 before a firm decision was taken to build, on the site at 'Drumartane', then owned by Mr John Giffard and Alderman Nathaniel Hone. An application for consent was made to Lord Viscount Fitzwilliam. At a meeting on 13 October 1813, it was announced that this had been granted, and that, agreement having been signalled by the majority of Protestant parishioners in a petition to the Lord Lieutenant and the Privy Council, the building would go ahead. An application was to be made to the Board of First Fruits, the body then responsible for church building, for a loan. This resulted, in 1815, in a loan of £4,332-1-9d.

The Vestry meeting of 2 May 1814 was informed that the loan had been approved. It would be repaid in instalments over seventeen years, this money to be raised by applottment at a rate of two shillings and three pence per acre per annum. It was decided that William Farrell, the Diocesan Architect, would prepare a revision of his original plans for the new church. Permission from the Privy Council was forthcoming in August 1815, and the basic plans regarding walls, roof, tower and spire were agreed, but decisions on interior fittings were deferred.

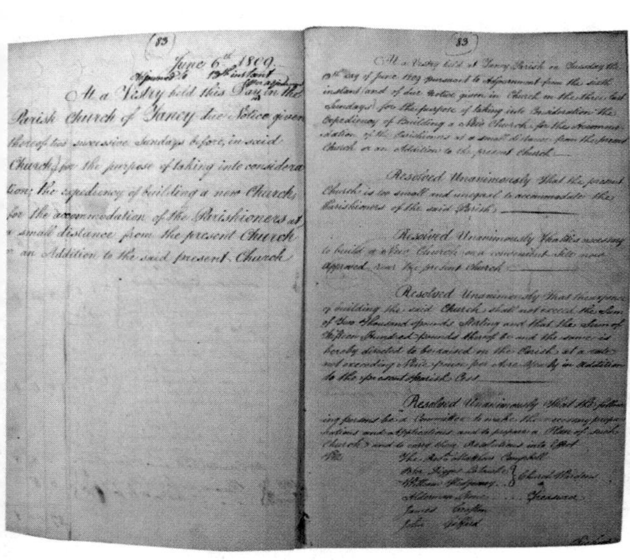
June 6th 1809.

At a Vestry held this Day in the Parish Church of Taney due Notice given thereof two successive Sundays before, in said Church, for the purpose of taking into consideration the expediency of building a new Church, for the accommodation of the Parishioners at a small distance from the present Church or an Addition to the said present Church

A Vestry Minute Book entry dated 6 June 1809, when the Select Vestry met to consider either 'the expediency of building a new church' or 'an addition to the said present church'.

Work was begun, but it soon became apparent that the amount of money raised by the loan from the Board of First Fruits would be insufficient. On 25 September 1816, it was resolved that money would be raised by the sale at auction of pew sites, purchasers to pay by instalments for the carpenters' work in fitting the actual pews. Failure to pay the appropriate instalments would result in forfeiture of the said pews. Owners could, if they wished, place an entry in the Vestry Book attaching the pew to their respective dwelling houses, and they, or their executors or administrators, could opt to reassign the pews to other residents. The seats were to be numbered in brass. At an auction held on 24 October 1816, the sale of eighteen pew sites on the ground floor and eight on the gallery raised the sum of £384-10-0. By 1817, it was estimated that the total sum required to complete the church would be £6,970-9-9, exceeding the original loan by £2,638-8-0. An application for another loan was made to the Board of First Fruits, but proved unsuccessful. Nevertheless, it was decided to open the church on Sunday, 21 June 1818, 'in consequence of His Grace the Archbishop of Cashel having granted

An old postcard featuring Christ Church Taney.

a license for the use of the new church previous to consecration'. (Vestry Minutes, 15 June 1818)

Although the church was now in use, it was far from complete, and the Parish found itself in considerable financial difficulty. In October 1820, an approach was made to the Archbishop of Cashel, who was standing in temporarily for the Archbishop of Dublin, 'but to which his Grace did not deem it necessary to answer'. (Vestry Minutes, 2 October 1820) The committee now realised that the Board of First Fruits was unlikely to provide a grant to cover the debts now due to various tradesmen who had been employed in the building and fitting out of the church. Protestant parishioners would now be asked to commit themselves to pay an additional rate, proportional to the value of their houses.

> *Should this proposition be acceded to your Committee do believe that the very best grounds would be laid for the parishioners entertaining the hope of having so severe a stigma on so wealthy a parish as that of suffering their just debts to remain undischarged speedily removed … They see no other means of an honourable removal of the difficulties with which the Parish is embarrassed, or of an honourable excuse for occupying a tabernacle erected to the service of God which may possibly lead to the ruin of those persons that undertook its construction in the confidence of being fully remunerated.*
> Vestry Minutes, 2 October 1820

Estimate for the Building of Taney Church

	£SD	£SD
Mason's work	2,350-15-1	
Carpenter's work	2,138-14-5	
Plasterer's work	298-4-0	
Stone Cutter's work	238-14-0	
Glaziers' and Painters' work	80-0-0	
Carvers' work	28-10-11	

Slaters' work	136-6-10	
Plumbers' work	23-11-3	
Iron mongers' work	31-19-10	
Erecting stoves	60-0-0	
Incidents	100-0-0	
Architect's charge	274-16-0	5761-12-4
A Bathstone Spire 64 feet high		
6 inches thick	320-0-0	
Ornament at top	25-0-0	
Architect's charge	17-5-0	362-5-0
One large and one small bell including wheel mounting etc.	136-0-0	
A large clock, dials etc.	110-0-0	
Surrounding walls	190-0-0	
Gate entrance and iron railing	300-0-0	
Forming and gravelling ground	100-0-0	
Cash paid by Architect for advertising	10-12-5	
	6,970-9-9	
Cash received from Board of First Fruits	4,322-1-9	
Cash received by sale of seats	1,500-0-0	
	5,832-1-9	
Sum required to complete the work	1,138-8-0	
William Farrell, Architect, February 1817		

The following decades saw the Parish struggle to fundraise and to pay for necessary improvements and repairs. The loan from the Board of First Fruits was never fully repaid – nine instalments were paid, but, following the passing of the Irish Church Temporalities Act (1833), the outstanding debt was cancelled. The church was not finally paid for until 1872, when Henry Roe, a prominent parishioner who had been church warden from 1864 to 1867, cleared the remaining liabilities prior to consecration.

Perusal of the Vestry minute books of the past two centuries provides a fascinating insight into the discussions carried on and the decisions taken concerning the building, extending, modernising and financing of Christ Church. We read, for example, of an application to Mr Charles Hawthorne, the Commissioner for Excise and Taxes, to have the window tax on the church partially commuted, and of some public opposition to this:

> *Resolved unanimously that the anonymous publication in the Hibernian Journal of the 10 Instant, and since republished in other newspapers, purporting to be a statement of the proceedings of our Vestry on Monday last on the subject of the said commutation, is an insidious and malignant misrepresentation of the proceedings of this parish on that occasion calculated to deceive his Majesty's Minister in his endeavours to collect the unbiased sense of the people.*
>
> Vestry Minutes, 13 October 1817

On Tuesday, 8 June 1824, it was resolved that the church wardens, Maurice Hime and Daniel Kinehan, be 'authorised to purchase a bell of the estimated weight of fine cut and that they be hereby authorised to draw sixty pounds from the Bank for the payment of said bell and for placing it in its proper situation in the Tower of the said Parish Church'. By April 1825, there was a problem of dampness in the church, and the estimate of £167-17-3d from William Moyens of Rathfarnham was to be accepted, 'the outside of the church to be carefully and securely covered with a material of Roman Cement, agreeable to the particular specification of the said estimate'. It was also resolved 'that the outside door of the church

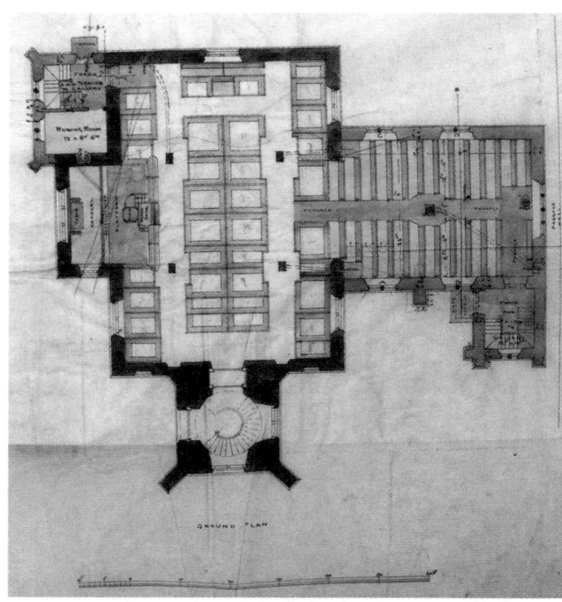

The plan for reconfiguring and extending Christ Church Taney, drawn by Welland and Gillespie and dated 10 March 1861, held by the RCB Library.

leading to the vestry room be built up with lime and stone in order to increase the comfort and warmth of the church and Vestry room'. (Vestry Minutes, 19 April 1825)

Several decades later, much work remained to be done. A document held by the library of the Representative Church Body, dated 10 July 1860, specifies work required for the enlarging of the church, to include:

1. Removing a portion of the wall on the south side, shoring up roof, making doorway to new robing room.
2. Erecting a transept on the south side.
3. Fitting up transept with benches and erecting a gallery therein.
4. Constructing a porch with staircase to gallery.
5. Altering and refitting pulpit and desk.
6. Altering chancel and providing new chancel rails.
7. Erecting a robing room and porch adjoining.
8. Making such further alterations as will be found necessary in the walls, roofs, floors, windows, fittings and passages to enable the works show, by plans to be executed.

The library also holds the 'Memorial for enlarging church', dated 29 January 1861, and the 'Draft Faculty for altering and enlarging church', dated 12 February 1861. The following years saw the building of the nave, the west gallery and the south porch, and a variety of internal adjustments. The 'Petition of Faculty to make alterations in Parish Church' (21 May 1869) includes plans to 'take up present pews and to repair church, place pulpit and desk in new positions, make change in chancel, reduce depth of galleries and repair them', while the 'Copy of Citation for Faculty to make alterations in Parish Church', dated 27 May 1869, proposes 'repairing the Centre of the Church, repairing the Galleries and changing the position of the Communion Table, Pulpit and reading desk'.

A small organ had been purchased by the Parish in 1844, costing £43-3-8d, but in 1871, an organ of higher quality, built by Forster and Andrews of Hull at a cost of £600, was presented to the church by Henry Roe. This was initially placed in the west gallery, but in 1930, it was moved and rebuilt in the chancel by Telfords. The new chancel and the east windows were also provided by the Roe family in 1872 and, as mentioned earlier, the outstanding debts on the church were paid off by Henry Roe, clearing the way for the Act of Consecration.

Christ Church Tawney – Act of Consecration Dated 10 June 1872

In the name of God Amen, Whereas a Church has been erected out of funds contributed for that purpose by several pious and well disposed persons, on a site in the parish of Tawney, in the county and Diocese of Dublin. And such church is adorned and furnished with all things decent and necessary for the worship of God. And whereas the incumbent, Church Wardens and Parishioners of the said Parish, have requested of us to separate the said church from all common and profane uses, and to consecrate the same. Therefore we, Richard Chevenix, by Divine Providence, Lord Archbishop of Dublin, willing to comply with their pious and religious desire, do forever separate the same from all common and profane uses, and do consecrate, devote and dedicate the said church to the worship of God, and celebration of Divine Service, and we ordain that from henceforth forever public prayer be openly read in the said Church according to the use of the Church of Ireland, the word of God sincerely preached, the Sacraments administered, and that all matters be done and performed, which by the laws of God and the Canons of the Church can, or may, be done towards Divine Worship, to the glory of God, and the edifying of the Church. And we ordain and constitute the said Church a Parochial Church to and for the use of the Parishioners of the Parish of Tawney forever hereafter with the privileges accustomed or competent to any parish church founded of old within the Diocese of Dublin, and we do consecrate the said Church to the honour of God and to Holy uses by the name of Christ Church Tawney, and we pronounce, decree and declare, that the same is consecrated and that it ought to remain so to future times, reserving nevertheless to ourselves and our successors Lords Archbishops of Dublin the power of visiting the said church when we or they shall think it our office so to do, in order that we may see that the same be taken care of in its repairs and ornaments, and that all things be observed therein canonically and orderly. All which we decree and confirm for us and our successors Archbishops of Dublin. Dated this tenth day of June, in the year of Our Lord One Thousand Eight Hundred and Seventy Two.

Richard Chevenix Dublin

The original petition for the consecration of Christ Church, 'to assign it perpetually to be a parochial church for the inhabitants of the said parish by the name of Christ Church', signed by the rector, William Alfred Hamilton, and church wardens Andrew Hayes and John Reilly, is retained in the Representative Church Body library, as is the Consecration Document, dated 10 June 1872. A lively description of the consecration ceremony appeared in the *Irish Times* of Tuesday, 11 June 1872:

The Consecration of Christ's Church, Taney

The ceremony of consecrating this beautiful edifice was performed yesterday by the Archbishop of Dublin. There were a number of clergy-men present, who took an interest in the proceedings. Amongst them were – The Rev Mr Hamilton, Vicar of the Parish, the Dean of the Chapel Royal, Rev Dr Gibbings, Rev Dr Wright, Rev P Walsh, Rev W Jellet, Rev Dr Ryder, Rev Mr Storey, Rev Dr Griffin, Rev James Walsh and Company. The petition praying the Archbishop to consecrate the Church was presented by the two Church Wardens, Mr Henry Roe and Mr Reilly. The usual ceremony was then gone through by the Archbishop and his Chaplains, after which a sermon was preached by His Grace suitable for the occasion. The Holy Communion was afterwards administered to about one hundred Communicants. The church has been for a number of years in existence, but it has just undergone a thorough renovation through the generous munificence of Mr Henry Roe, he having at his own expense, erected a new chancel, and furnished a new organ. It has been up to this time used only for worship under a licence from the Archbishop, but the parishioners had thought this a fitting opportunity to have it consecrated, which was done under the most favourable circumstances. The church is situated in the midst of a beautiful country, prettily studded with trees and well watered: the day was on the whole very fine, a few slight showers occurring at intervals but not sufficient to mar the success of the interesting ceremony. There were a number of parishioners present, and others who had been invited to an 'at home' at his handsome residence, Mount Anville Park, where a magnificent entertainment was provided, at which about two hundred and fifty were present.

The Irish Times, Tuesday 11 June 1872

Christ Church was now officially the Parish church of Taney, but the next 120 years were to continue to witness many changes. The year 1878 saw the leasing from the Earl of Pembroke of further land to the east of the church for 150 years, at a rent of one shilling per year.

New gates were added to the east and to the front of the church grounds. In 1898, the church was valued for insurance purposes at £4,500, including the stained glass windows, with the fittings considered to be worth £1,000 and the organ £500. The annual premium was around £3. By contrast, in 2013, Christ Church Taney is insured for €7,216,351, the total Parish property is insured for €10,015,226 and the insurance premium alone costs nearly €38,000 (including government levy) per annum.

The impressive brass eagle that gazes out across the church.

Further improvements and renovations took place throughout the twentieth century, together with the acquisition of a fine selection of artefacts. In 1902, for example, the Parish purchased a safe in which to keep the church silver and a flag for the flagstaff on the church tower, while a gift was received, from the Hamilton family, of a brass eagle lectern. The following year, a new bell was ordered.

At the time of the one-hundredth anniversary of the opening of the church for worship, Reverend Monk Gibbon had ambitious plans.

In 1918, as now, there was a constant need to raise money. The then rector pointed out that if their predecessors could raise over £5,000 to build the new church, then it should not be beyond the capacity of parishioners in 1918 to raise £500.

There were three things the Parish desired to achieve: to replace the Holy Communion flagon with a silver one, bearing a suitable inscription; to wipe out a debt of £110; and to move the organ (then in the west gallery) to the chancel and south transept. The idea to move the organ had originated just before the outbreak of the First World War, and Monk Gibbon believed that 'these plans should be carried into effect as soon as reasonably possible as a proper and fitting celebration of the centenary of the Parish church. In the opinion of musical experts it would greatly benefit the organ and improve the praise of our public worship, while it would, with the opening of the west window, give the light to the church originally intended and provided for when the nave was built.'

The first two plans were to be effected immediately, and the moving of the organ when the war ended. A large committee was formed, and a Centenary Fund was set up. Money raised included £12-15-0d from a concert and lecture, £10-0-0d from a school concert, £14-11-4d from 'dramatic entertainment' and £2-0-0d from a jumble sale. Mrs Williams Barrington allowed the Vestry to hold the summer fête in the grounds of her home, Eden Park. Added to this were subscriptions totalling £36-4-0d, along with 'special subscriptions', bringing the total fairly quickly up to £241-6-4d. A special offertory collection on Sunday, 23 June, raised the necessary £14-10-0d for the silver flagon. The congregation of St Thomas's Church in Foster Avenue presented a silver Holy Communion casket, costing £3.

The later moving of the organ to the chancel, after twenty years of discussion (!), cost £388-0-0d. The church was wired for electricity in 1929, and by 1947 required complete rewiring. The church grounds were planted, developed and maintained largely thanks to the generosity of the Overend Family, and in 1970, plans were approved for the building of the Overend extension, a small room used as Parish office, storeroom and Sunday creche for two decades. This was demolished to make way for the entrance to the new Parish Centre.

The 150th anniversary of the dedication of the church was also celebrated, with a special service held at 8pm on Friday, 21 June 1968. The preacher was the Archbishop of Dublin, George Otto Simms, and the lessons were read by former curates of Taney:

This photograph gives a sense of the work involved in refurbishing a 200-year-old church.

Reverend T.S. Hopwell, Rector of St Thomas's, Mount Merrion, and Reverend R.G. Hipwell McCollum, Rector of Clontarf.

As time went on, normal wear and tear, as well as repairs to the roof and heating system and problems with woodwork and dry rot, continued to be a drain on Parish resources. This culminated in the late 1980s in a major restoration and redecoration job, at a total cost, as given in the Treasurer's Report of 26 April 1990, of £186,000. The organ was also rebuilt, at a cost of £54,000. Further major work on the roof again proved necessary in 1993, costing £36,989. Doubtless, meeting the costs of maintenance of the church fabric will always tax the ingenuity of Parish fundraisers.

In 1981, a new church clock was provided in memory of parishioner Miss Letitia Overend (1880–1977), and a marble tablet at the top of the tower stairs marks this gift.

In 1991, the side chapel, known as the 'Barbara Chapel' after Mrs Barbara Coote (née Eaton, 1917–87), whose husband Michael provided for the alterations in commemoration of his wife, was formed in the southeast corner of the nave. This, in addition to the baptistery, has been used along with the chancel for the serving of Holy Communion.

In 1997, a parishioner, the late Norah Boyce, left a gift of €500 to the Parish. This was used to buy a brass handrail for the chancel steps, which her family agreed was an appropriate memorial to her. Around this time, antennae for the provision of broadband were placed on the roof of Christ Church, in exchange for an annual fee, providing broadband services to Parish buildings.

At the very end of 1999, the bells from St George's Church were installed in the tower of Christ Church Taney. They were rung on New Year's Eve 1999 to celebrate the new millennium, and they ring out every Sunday to welcome us to church. A plaque in the tower porch tells us that these bells were first rung in St George's Church on 1 January 1829 and first rung in Christ Church Taney

The beautiful, warm and serene interior of Christ Church Taney.

on 1 January 2000. At the top of the stairs above the porch sits the Feisters Bell of 1719. A short chapter about the bells follows this one.

Major renovations were carried out again in 2006. The church was closed for major repairs to the leaking roof and replacement of loose slates, which were causing a risk to safety. While this was happening, church services took place in the Parish Centre. In his report to the Easter General Vestry on 26 April 2006, Reverend Desmond Sinnamon described the work to be done, in five phases:

Phase 1: Re-roofing of the oldest (1818) section was underway.

Phase 2: Re-slating and insulation of the remainder of the church was in progress.

Phase 3: The ornate ceiling was to be strengthened by stainless steel pins at intervals across its span. The ceiling would then be redecorated, as would the church as a whole.

Phase 4: The outsides of the windows would be repaired and painted, and repairs carried out on the church tower.

Phase 5: The former sexton's cottage would be newly slated and timbers replaced.

All of this, he believed, 'would lead to a warmer, safer church'. The final cost of this work was €506,327.95 for Christ Church, €40,621.43 for the cottage and €2,043.00 for the removal of a tree. At the same time as this, €18,579.95 was required for repairs to St Nahi's Church. This huge expenditure was alleviated slightly by a grant of €20,000 from Dun Laoghaire–Rathdown County Council, and another of €10,000 from the Marshall Beresford Fund. Nevertheless, these sums indicate the burden on Church of Ireland parishes of repair and maintenance of their historic buildings.

In recent times, a consciousness has grown of the day-to-day problems faced by people with disabilities, and the importance of the small actions that can be taken to enable everyone to participate in social and community activities. In consideration of this, it was decided in January 2008 to remove some pews to make space for wheelchairs.

Meanwhile, in 2011, the Parish addressed the provision of sound systems in the Parish buildings, to give better access to people with significant hearing loss. The Christ Church microphone and induction loop system, first installed in 1995, was overhauled and a new amplifier and extra microphones were added. At the same time, new systems were installed in St Nahi's Church, the Overend Room and the Minor Hall, where there had been none before, and a loop was added to the Main Hall. The cost was covered by a bequest.

In 2017, as part of the celebrations of 200 years of worship in the church, a full renovation was carried out. Pews were removed from the front of the nave to allow for more flexibility of use during services, and for concerts and similar events. A retractable screen was installed for audio–visual use. The choir pews were removed and replaced with modern choir chairs, and reinforced-glass screens were added to the front of the balconies to prevent falls. The whole building was beautifully painted in modern colours, and a new carpet was laid. The church's ambience is now, once again, one of a warm, comfortable, contemporary and welcoming space for worship.

The Curate's Cottage.

* * *

Christ Church Taney is set well back from Taney Road, and within the grounds to either side of the main entrance gates are two cottages, which are believed to have been built shortly after the opening of the church. Church Lodge was purpose-built to house the sexton, while Church Cottage was used during the nineteenth century as an

Christ Church Taney seen from the air.

Every year, a Christmas tree is erected on the top of the church tower, visible from all over Dundrum.

infants' school. In February 1903, two years after the infants' school was amalgamated with the boys' and girls' school in 1901, the sexton moved across to the former school cottage. The second cottage then provided housing for the Parish curate. For periods during the twentieth and twenty-first centuries, it was rented out to private individuals, but it then reverted to being a curate's house. As the Parish no longer employs a sexton, the former sexton's house is currently rented out to tenants.

Straight ahead is the church itself, built in early-nineteenth-century Gothic revival style. The most prominent feature is the square bell tower, housing the St George's bells. At the time of writing of the 1994 Parish history, the bells could be accessed by way of a series of three tall and very rickety ladders. There were rungs missing, and one ladder balanced on a beer barrel! Nowadays, much safer ladders provide access.

At the top of the third ladder, a trap door leads out on to the roof of the tower, whence can be seen magnificent views of Dundrum and its environs. A turret on one corner of the tower is inscribed: 'To the Glory of God and in memory of my beloved husband James

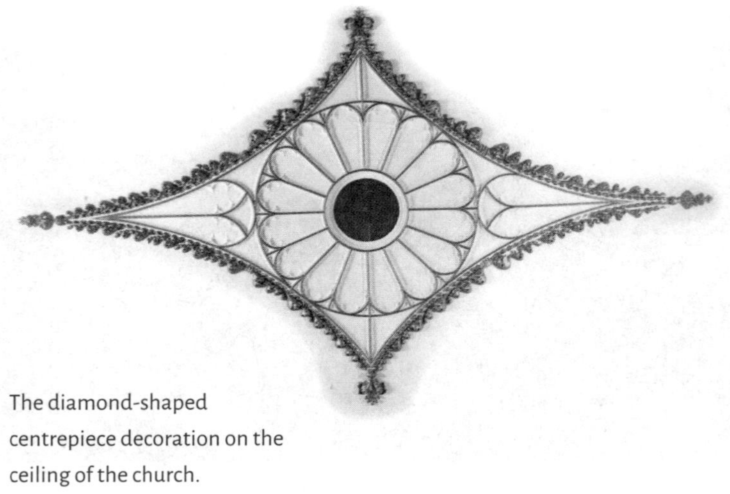

The diamond-shaped centrepiece decoration on the ceiling of the church.

Sheill who died 28 March 1921.' Another carries the inscription: 'In memory of John George Gibbon and Mary Eleanor his wife.'

This tower constitutes a landmark that can be seen from right across Dundrum, particularly at Christmas when a tree is erected and illuminated at the top.

The church is in a cruciform shape, although originally it was merely formed from the rectangle of the nave, without transepts, and with a shallow recess to the east containing the communion table. It was Henry Roe, who in 1871 had presented the organ, who provided for the erection of the chancel in 1872, and the windows there are dedicated to the Roe family.

The west end of the church has random rubble walling and a steeply sloped slate roof. The chancel is in coursed block work, again with slate roof. To the east of the church sits the Parish Centre, of which more later.

Taney's carved stone baptismal font.

If one enters the west door, one will see to the right a timber staircase leading to the west balcony. On the north wall here there is a clear glass window. At the top of the stairs is a timber-partitioned area. This once had a door, but it has been removed. Passing through a pair of timber doors set in a pointed-arched opening, one enters the west balcony, which has five steps with four tiers of seating. In the west wall is set a large window featuring Gothic revival tracery; the glass panes are clear.

Back on ground level, from the west porch, double timber doors, set in a pointed-arched opening on the left, lead into the main church. An internal porch has been created with a glazed screen. Here church hymnals and prayer books are kept for offering to visitors. On the opposite side of the rear of the church is another screened-off alcove, open-fronted and containing a high-backed pew and book-shelving.

From the west, the nave extends to the crossing point of the transepts, with a timber-trussed roof of graceful simplicity. The two trusses, of very slender proportions and featuring some basic tracery, spring from delicate stone corbels. Between these are additional trusses formed by cross-bracing timbers. The walls of the nave are pierced by two gothic arched windows on each side, two clear and two in stained glass. There is fixed pew seating, with a central aisle running the length of the church up to the altar.

Dr David Adams at the organ.

At the crossing point, the roof changes to a flat, plastered ceiling with a beautifully ornate cornice, presently painted white, gold and red. The centrepiece of this ceiling is a diamond shape, its decorative motifs and tracery picked out in gold against a white background. The effect at this crossing point is of a large rectangular shape, of which the axis is at right angles to the nave, and this forms the dominant space within the church, with additional aisles on each side.

Facing each other across this space are two timber panel-fronted balconies, supported by slender cast-iron columns. Access to the south balcony is via a timber cranked staircase leading from the southernmost aisle. This staircase was dedicated as a memorial to Canon Orr in October 1966, when six collecting plates were given to the church by Canon Orr's widow and family. The north balcony is reached by an elegant stone spiral staircase, housed in the porch under the bell tower.

Above: Taney altar.

Left: A detail of plasterwork on the ceiling.

The pulpit is located to the north of the nave. It is octagonal in shape, of heavily carved stone set on a black marble plinth, with black marble columns set around the base and green marble columns around the main body. Red marble bosses are set around the top. Each facet is inscribed with religious text, and around the base is the inscription 'Give until the Lord the Glory due unto his name'. Beside this is the baptistery with its carved stone font.

Its match on the opposite side is the Coote side chapel. To the right of this is a door leading to the Parish Centre, while to its left is the rector's prayer desk, dedicated to the memory of Catherine Mary James, in a similar carved stone and marble style to the pulpit, but square in shape. There is a lectern, given in memory of William Alfred Hamilton DD – a magnificent brass eagle with outspread wings sits upon a ball on top of a spiral-fluted column. On its base sit three brass lions in repose.

The chancel, with its timber-trussed roof and tiled floor, is entered under a high Gothic arch. On either side are the choir stalls, while on the south wall is the Forster and Andrews organ. When this fine two-manual instrument was moved from the west gallery to its present position in 1930, it was converted to pneumatic action. In 1989, the organ was rebuilt as new by Kenneth Jones & Associates of Bray, at a cost of £50,000, and restored to its original tracker action. The current organist is Dr David Adams.

The carved timber altar is beyond the choir area, in a narrower end bay. During church services, a silver cross, which was dedicated on 21 November 1965, is normally placed behind the altar. The altar rail, given in memory of Margaret H. Kinahan of Roebuck Park in 1929, projects out into the chancel and is splayed at each end. The altar itself is at the extreme east end, beyond a smaller Gothic arch, which is in part supported by columns resting on large corbels. The archway is further emphasised by a moulding, tracing the shape of the arc and terminating in bosses of carved leaves. There are narrow windows on the north and south walls, containing stained glass commemorating members of the Roe family, and the major five-panelled east window above the altar has fine tracery, including a rose feature at the top. It is dedicated to Mr and Mrs Henry Roe of Mount Anville, generous benefactors to the Parish, and dated 1872. Beyond the organ on the south wall of the chancel is the door leading to the Vestry room.

The church contains many memorial plaques and windows of interest. In the north porch is a plaque to George Kinahan DL, 1903, dedicating the bell to his memory; one commemorating the erection of the church clock by Letitia Overend in 1981; one stating the the porch table was given by friends of Katherine Lillian Moeran in 1964; and one stating that the floor was relaid in the memory of Sarah Gilbert and Margaret Wheatley.

Within the church itself, on the north wall is a plaque to Francis Stuart Verschoyle and William Arthur Verschoyle, who died in the First World War.

On the north wall of the rectangular area is a marble memorial plaque to William Alfred Hamilton, Rector of Taney from 1867 to 1895, and one to Edward Alma Stanley, Sexton, who died in 1917. A window on the east wall above the

The Taney Great War Memorial.

north balcony, representing the Good Shepherd, is to the memory of William Goulding, 1817–84, formerly MP of Cork.

The south wall opposite is the site of a number of interesting memorials. There is a brass memorial plaque set on black granite, in memory of Reverend Edward Arnold Carroll, Curate, who died in 1896. On the staircase to the south balcony is one to Adrian William Fielder Orr, Rector of Taney from 1935 to 1958, to whom the staircase was dedicated on 2 October 1966. Further along the south wall is a memorial to William Steward Collen, and another to Henrietta Catherine Hamilton, wife of Reverend William Alfred Hamilton. The latter appears to have been moved from the other side of the church, since the inscription reads, 'This Brass is placed beneath his monument by their Children'. There is a stone plaque to Olive Kinahan (1936), and a brass one to Everard Hamilton of Ballinteer Lodge (died 1925), his wife Elinor, their son Gustavus and their daughter, Helen. Everard Hamilton was a church warden from 1883 to 1887. A solicitor, he assisted Francis Elrington Ball in the writing of the first history of Taney Parish in 1895.

The Armenian community in Ireland now holds its church services and Sunday School in Taney, and in the chancel hangs a banner representing the 'Armenian Apostolic Parish Church Dublin'.

Here is a description of the windows in Christ Church Taney:

Sanctuary, east: Five lancets (1872) (William Holland Studio, Warwick)

- Left lower: King Solomon Building the Temple
- Left upper: Mass in the Bullrushes
- Second: Moses and the Brazen Serpent
- Centre: Elijah Ascending to Heaven
- Fourth: Abraham Sacrificing Isaac
- Right lower: King Solomon in the Temple
- Right upper: Moses and the Tables of the Law

Some of the spectacular windo[illegible]f Christ Church Taney

Sanctuary, north: One lancet (*c.*1872) (William Holland Studio)

- Visiting the Sick

Sanctuary, south: One lancet (*c.*1872) (William Holland Studio)

- Visiting the Prisoner

Chancel, north, east-most: Two lancets (*c.*1872) (William Holland Studio)

- Left: Taking in the Stranger
- Right: Clothing the Naked

Chancel, north, west-most: Two lancets (*c.*1872) (William Holland Studio)

- Left: Feeding the Hungry
- Right: Giving Drink to the Thirsty

North transept, east: One lancet (1884) (attributed to Mayer & Co. of Munich)

- Christ as Good Shepherd

Nave, north, east-most: Two lancets (1908) (Clayton & Bell Studio, London, and cartoonist George Daniels)

- Left: Wisdom
- Right: Hope

Nave, south, east-most: Two lancets (1905) (Clayton & Bell Studio and George Daniels)

- Left: Faith
- Right: Charity

Nave, south, west-most: Two lancets (1994) (Michael Judd)

- Road to Emmaus

A detail from the 'Road to Emmaus' window.

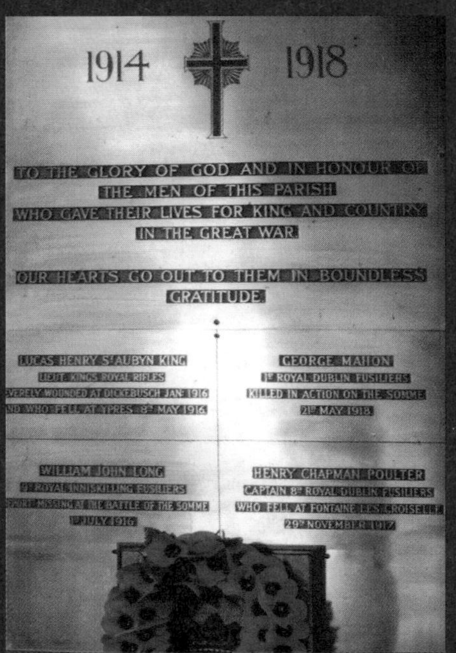

TO THE GLORY OF GOD AND IN HONOUR OF THE MEN OF THIS PARISH WHO GAVE THEIR LIVES FOR KING AND COUNTRY IN THE GREAT WAR.

OUR HEARTS GO OUT TO THEM IN BOUNDLESS GRATITUDE.

Each of these windows has a dedication to a former Parish member or rector, either within the window itself or on an adjacent plaque.

The 'Road to Emmaus' is the one modern window in the church, having been dedicated on 16 October 1994 by the Archbishop of Dublin, Dr Donald Caird, in memory of Canon Walton Burrows, Rector of Taney from 1959 to 1983. It depicts Jesus joining the disciples walking from Jerusalem on the Road to Emmaus. Interestingly, it has been suggested by the Burrows family that one of the disciples depicted is a woman, and that this reflects the open and far-seeing mind of Canon Burrows in relation to the Church he loved and served. This window cost £8,000, half of which was paid by the family and half by voluntary subscription plus an anonymous donation.

On the chancel's north wall is the large brass memorial to those from the Parish who perished in the First World War. Twenty men are honoured here, with details of when and where they died, and it makes harrowing reading.

Details on each man were kindly provided by the Royal Dublin Fusiliers Association. They are as follows:

1. Erik de Berg, died 21 March 1918 – Private, 7th Battalion Royal Irish Regiment; born in Monkstown, County Dublin; enlisted in Dundrum; killed in action in France in the last German offensive of the war.
2. Thomas Augustus Carey, died 5 December 1917 – 2nd Lieutenant, 1st Battalion Irish Guards; killed in action in France; his name is on the Thiepval Memorial at the Somme.
3. William Stewart Collen, died 7 August 1915 – Lieutenant, 6th Battalion Royal Inniskilling Fusiliers; son of Joseph and Hanna Collen of 'Homestead' Dundrum; killed at age 25 in action at Gallipoli; buried in Green Hill Cemetery, Turkey; named on Special Memorial, A.5.
4. Arthur Chichester Crookshank, died 16 August 1915 – Sergeant 7th Battalion, 'D' Company, The Pals, Royal Dublin Fusiliers; born in Dublin; educated at Mr Strangeways School and St Columba's College Dublin, law student at Trinity College Dublin and solicitor's apprentice; captain of 1st xv rugby team and winner of Ballinteer Cup For All-Round Sport at St Columba's; made a sergeant on August 9 1915, missing at Gallipoli a week later; no known grave; name on the Helles Memorial, Turkey.

5. John Robert Earl, died 26 March 1918 – Private, 4th (Queen's Own) Huzzars; killed in action at age 49; husband of Margaret Earl of 265 Corporation Buildings, Nicholas Street, Dublin; no known grave; name on Posieres Memorial at the Somme.
6. Frederick Richard Earl, died 9 February 1919 – Inniskilling Fusiliers; not included in the register of 'soldiers died in the war', presumably because he died shortly after the end of the war.
7. Arthur George Jameson, died 23 November 1914 – Lieutenant Commander, Royal Navy.
8. Harold Gordon Jameson, died 16 August 1915 – 2nd Lieutenant, 65th Field Company, Royal Engineers; killed in action at age 26; son of Robert William and Katherine Anne Jameson of 'Ardanoir', Greystones, County Wicklow; educated at Monkton Combe School, Bath, and Trinity College, Dublin; appointed an Assistant Director of Works in the Sudan Irrigation Service in 1911; no known grave; name on the Helles Memorial, Turkey.
9. Lucas Henry St. Aubyn King, died 8 May 1916 – Lieutenant, 2nd Battalion, King's Royal Rifle Corps; killed in action in France; name on the Ypres (Menin Gate) Memorial in Belgium.
10. William John Long, died 1 July 1916 – Private, Royal Inniskilling Fusiliers; born and enlisted in Dublin; killed in action at the Somme offensive; no known grave; name on the Thiepval Memorial at the Somme.
11. George Mahon, died 21 May 1918 – Private, 1st Battalion, Royal Dublin Fusiliers; died of wounds, aged 25; only son of John and Annie Mahon of 37 Ballalley Cottages, Dundrum; buried in Cinq Rues British Cemetery Nord (Grave no. 22).
12. Henry Chapman Poulter, died 29 November 1917 – Captain, 8th Battalion, Royal Dublin Fusiliers; killed in action, aged 23; son of Henry C. Poulter of St. Brigid's, Roebuck, Clonskeagh, Co. Dublin; buried in St. Leger British Cemetery – Pas de Calais (Grave no. H5).

13. William Forman Poulter, died 6 March 1918 – 2nd Lieutenant, 24th Squadron, Royal Flying Corps; killed in combat, aged 19; brother of Henry Chapman Poulter, above; buried in Honnechy British Cemetery Nord (Grave no. IIDI4).
14. Walter Wrixon de Rossiter, died 12 October 1917 – Captain, 42nd Battalion, Canadian Infantry, Quebec Regiment; Mentioned In Despatches; died of wounds received at Vimy Ridge, aged 49; son of Thomas and Annie de Rossiter of Dundrum; husband of Catherine Frances de Rossiter of 8 Temple Villas, Palmerston Road, Dublin; served in the South African campaign; buried in Aubigny Communal Cemetery Extension (Grave no.VI.H.II).
15. Thomas Ernest Saunders, died 8 June 1915 – Private, 'B' Company, Wellington Regiment, N.Z.E.F.; killed in action 29 April 1915 (N.B. discrepancy between date on Taney memorial of 8 June and that supplied by the R.D.F.A.); son of Mrs F.A. and the late J. Saunders of Sydenham, Dundrum; no known grave; name on Lone Pine Memorial in Gallipoli (No. 76).
16. Isaac William Ussher, died 4 July 1916 – Lieutenant, 2nd Battalion, Royal Irish Regiment; killed in action at the Somme; name on the Thiepval Memorial at the Somme.
17. Francis Stewart Verschoyle, died 25 April 1915 – 2nd Lieutenant, 2nd Siege Company, Royal Engineers; killed in action at Hill 60, aged 19; son of W.H. and Frances Verschoyle of Woodley, Dundrum; buried in Ypres Town Cemetery (Grave No. G7).
18. William Arthur Verschoyle, died 11 April 1917 – Captain, 1st Battallion, Royal Irish Fusiliers, 87th Foot; killed in action, aged 27; brother of Francis Stewart Verschoyle, above; no known grave; name on the Arras Memorial, Pas de Calais.
19. Percival Westby, died 23 September 1917 – Lieutenant, 'A' Battery, 295th Brigade; killed in action on the Cambridge Road during the Third Battle of Ypres, aged 28; son of Francis and Louise

Westby of Roebuck Castle, Co. Dublin; buried in Brandhoek New Military Cemetery No. 3, Belgium (Grave No. I.H.16).

20. Henry Charles Wiseman, died 16 August 1916 – Rifleman, 1st Battalion, Royal Irish Rifles; born in Monaghan, enlisted in Dublin; killed in action near Messine Ridge [another discrepancy, with the Taney memorial saying he died at the Battle of the Somme]; no known grave; name on the Tynecot Memorial, Belgium.

The sacrifices of these men and the many millions of others who gave their lives in war are recognised every year in Taney with the solemn celebration of Remembrance Sunday, when a wreath is laid at the foot of this memorial.

* * *

Today, Christ Church Taney is a place of community, welcome and mutual support. This is enhanced by the less formal and friendlier approaches of clergy and parishioners alike, while the recent renovation symbolises a church being cherished and respected by all, and ready for service in its third century of worship.

Alan and Roger helping out.

CHAPTER 6

ST GEORGE'S BELLS

On 1 January 2000, Taney Parish welcomed the new millennium with the first peal in Taney of the magnificent bells that had been moved from St George's Church in Hardwicke Place, on the north side of Dublin city centre. These bells had first been heard on 1 January 1829 at the Church of St George, which at that time served what was numerically the largest parish in the Dublin Diocese, as Taney is today.

The set of eight bells had been cast by Mears of London in 1825, at a cost of 1,500 guineas, and presented by the architect Francis Johnston and his wife Anne in 1828 to a church opened for worship in 1814.

The inscriptions on the bells, which the Taney 1999 brochure tells us were recorded by the renowned campanologist (bell ringer), and member of St George's Change Ringers, Fred Dukes in his 1994 book *Campanology in Ireland*, are:

1. Treble – God save the king
2. Universal benevolence
3. God preserve the church. Amen
4. Peace and prosperity in Ireland
5. We rejoice to ring for our constitution and king
6. The Rev. W. Bushe M.A., Rector, the Rev. F. Bridge, the Rev. J. Short, Curates
7. Glory to God in the highest and on earth peace goodwill towards men

Bringing in the bells.

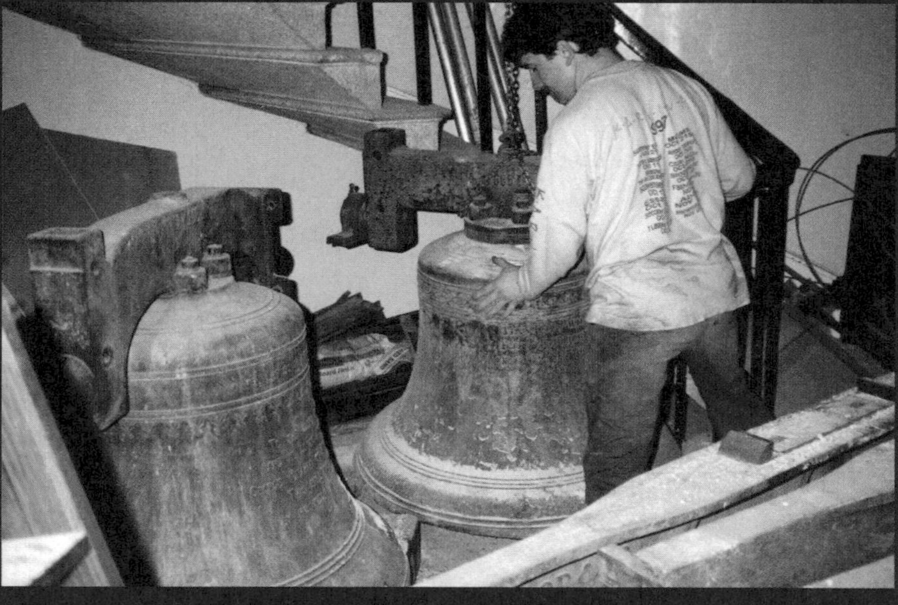

St George's Bells in the porch of Taney church.

8. We were all cast by Thomas Mears of London and presented to the parish of St. George's, Dublin by Francis Johnston, Architect of said church and Mrs. Anne Johnstone, his wife, 1828

These bells became a cherished part of Dublin's heritage, and were mentioned by James Joyce in *Ulysses*. Sadly, population movement and huge and unachievable projected costs for renovation and refurbishment resulted in St George's church closing in 1990, the final service with bells being held on 21 April 1990.

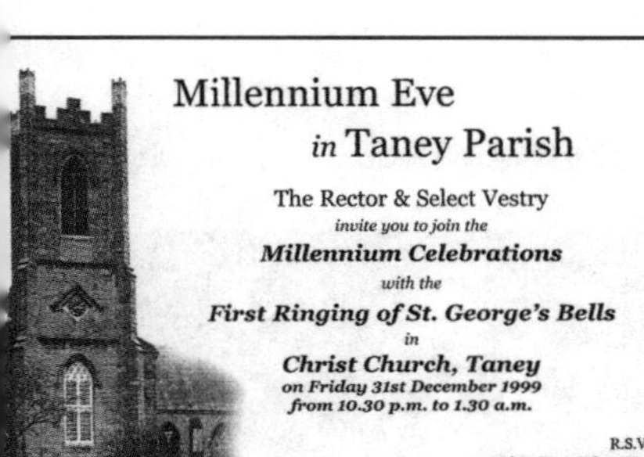

As the *Evening Herald* of 30 April 1990 described it, 'Last amens echo at St. George's'. However, the precious and much-loved bells were saved. They were carefully dismantled and removed before the sale of the church took place. The bells were put into storage, paid for in part by a generous donation from Bell's Shipping. When the ongoing cost became too much of a burden, Taney parishioner George Cooke provided safe and free storage at a warehouse in Bluebell industrial estate for over a decade, until Taney Parish was ready to hang them.

To Celebrate the
Third Millennium of Faith
The eight bells from St. George's Church,
(closed 1990)
were installed in Christ Church, Taney
through the generosity of:
PARISHIONERS OF TANEY
THE PARISH OF ST. GEORGE AND ST. THOMAS
TREVOR BROOKS & FAMILY
THE MILLAR FAMILY
OVEREND FAMILY TRUST OF AIRFIELD
THE NATIONAL MILLENNIUM COMMITTEE
CANON A. W. F. ORR IN MEMORIAM
ELIZABETH CURTIS IN MEMORIAM
THE IRISH ASSOCIATION OF CHANGE RINGERS
THE COMMUNITY OF DUNDRUM AND BEYOND
First Ring - St. George's - 1 Jan. 1829
First Ring - Christ Church Taney - 1 Jan. 2000
The belfry of George's Church sent out constant peals....
James Joyce

Above left: An invitation to the Millenium Eve celebrations, and the first ringing of St George's bells in Christ Church Taney.
Left: A commemorative plaque, complete with a quote from James Joyce.

Since Christ Church Taney was opened in 1818, just four years after St George's, it seemed appropriate for the bells to be installed there. However, the cost of preparing the tower and hanging the bells was estimated at around €64,000 and having just built the Parish Centre, the Parish had no available funds. Accordingly, a committee was set up in September 1997 to raise money, and a public appeal was launched in May 1999.

Planning permission was not required to install the bells, and the proposed installation met all relevant by-law approval. Structural engineers confirmed that the tower was structurally sound to take them. A fully sound-proofed ringing room would be built, so that

Top: Three helpful parishioners lend a hand with the bells.

Above: The Taney Change Ringers Society.

practising would not be heard outside the church. It was agreed that the bells would be rung only for services and on special occasions, to ensure minimum disturbance to residents of the neighbourhood.

On 31 May 1999, a reception was held for parishioners to announce 'A Millennium Opportunity' to sponsor the installation. This was attended by over 100 people, including the Archbishop of Dublin Dr Walton Empey, Minister of State Seamus Brennan and local councillors. The generosity of parishioners, local businesses and the public was supplemented by a substantial government grant from the Millennium Fund. The target was reached before the end of the year, and so the project could go ahead.

Meanwhile, another, even older, bell was transferred to Taney. The 'Felsters bell' had been stored in the belfry of St George's for many years. It had been presented by George Felsters in 1719 to an earlier St George's church, known as 'Little St George's', which had stood in Hill Street. When this church closed in 1894, the bell had been moved to St George's in Hardwicke Street. It was gifted to Taney by the parishioners of St George and St Thomas, and now sits at the top of the north gallery stairs of Christ Church Taney.

The installation of the eight bells was completed just in time to ring in the new millennium on New Year's Eve 1999/1 January 2000, and an estimated 1,000 people gathered at the church to celebrate the first peal of the bells at Taney. Canon Desmond Sinnamon and Reverend Bernadette Daly led the prayers and proceedings, and Father Donal O'Doherty, Parish Priest of Dundrum, and Reverend Tom Kingston, the Methodist Minister in Ballinteer, were among those who attended.

Cyril Galbraith, the first Ringing Master of the newly formed Taney Change Ringers Society, led the bell ringers from Taney and St George's up to the tower and, for the first time in a decade, the old bells rang out, just on the stroke of midnight. Fireworks and a night of festivities followed to celebrate the marvellous achievement of the saving and rehanging of these invaluable bells.

On Sunday, 26 November 2000, Archbishop Empey conducted a service of dedication for the bells. Subsequently, a tablet was erected in the church porch 'to celebrate the third millenium of faith', and to record with gratitude the generosity of the donors. A board has also been erected in the foyer of the Parish Centre, listing donors.

However, the pealing of the St George's bells for worship on Sundays by the Taney Change Ringers, and the joy it brings to us, is the real monument to the inspiration, work and funding behind this wonderful millennium project.

CHAPTER 7

THE CHAPEL OF EASE (1859–1956) IN MOUNT MERRION

During the nineteenth century, and particularly in winter, families living on the outer boundaries of the Parish did not find it easy to travel to church, and representations were made to the rector for permission to hold a Sunday evening service in Mount Merrion. A formal application to the church authorities was made by the Reverend Edward Busteed Moeran, followed up by a letter to a Mr Samuels, dated 23 April 1859, asking that such a service be allowed:

In a distant part of the Parish – A room has been fitted up at an expense of £30 and the families in that locality have offered to subscribe £30 towards a Curate.

My Curate, Mr Haddock, is quite willing to undertake the Service without any salary, but I thought it better, as a test of the sincerity of the applicants, to require some subscription. [Curiously, the curate Mr. Haddock is not mentioned in Leslie's Succession List, which is reproduced on pages 103 to 106.] *We wish to try the experiment for 12 months, in order to see how it succeeds ... I should like to commence if possible, on 1st Sunday in May ... I shall send to the Palace between 3 and 4 o'clock for your answer ...*

The licence was issued by the Archbishop of Dublin on 27 April 1859, and services began the following Sunday in the aforementioned room, in a cottage in the grounds of 'Seafield' on the Stillorgan Road, owned by Thomas Crozier.

By 1873, the cottage was too small for the numbers attending and the decision was taken to build a church – the third church within the Parish. The Earl of Pembroke granted a site at the corner of Foster Avenue and Stillorgan Road, and also subscribed £100 towards the building fund. The church, now known as St Thomas's but then described as the 'Chapel of Ease', cost £850, an amount which was fully covered by the subscriptions raised. In November 1874, the Reverend Alfred Hamilton petitioned for a licence. This was granted, and the opening service was held on Thursday, 3 December 1874.

The original plot on which the church stood was held 'in fee simple' under the deed of trust dated 31 December 1874. It was held by the trustees as a 'chapel of ease' to the Parish church of Taney, 'for the use and convenience of the parishioners of the said parish, and for the due performance therein of Divine Service according to the Articles, Liturgy and Rites of the Church of Ireland'. A further plot was added in April 1927, under a lease for 500 years from 25 March 1926, subject to a yearly rent of £12-10-0d, while the grounds were again extended in August 1936. In 1937, the Select Vestry decided that all three plots would be vested in the Representative Church Body by means of a conveyance, under Section 3 of the Glebe Land Representative Church Body Ireland Act 1835. The Representative Church Body acceded to this, subject to the Parish's agreement to pay the £12-10-0d annual rent.

An approach was made to the Parish during the same year by the County Council, who wished to obtain part of the church grounds

Confirmation with Bishop Walton Empey

to facilitate the widening of the Stillorgan Road. A sum of £50 in compensation was offered, but the Select Vestry decided to reject this and to go instead to arbitration. This was not entirely successful, as the Arbitration Court decided on compensation of only £55.

By 1940, discussions were well under way concerning the possibility of building a parochial hall for St Thomas's, at an estimated cost of £2,500. The Select Vestry put it to the Representative Church Body that, as they already owned the site and had collected £350 in subscriptions, which they hoped would increase to £500, the Representative Church Body might consider offering a grant.

The Representative Church Body's initial response was not encouraging. They wrote back, stating that if a grant was to be made, the difference between the sum required and the sum available would have to be considerably reduced, and that in any case, they would not make a grant until after the war. A loan of £2,000 was, however, subsequently approved, allowing the hall to be built at a cost of £2,672, and a grant of £50 was eventually made in February 1942 to help offset the loan. The Monk Gibbon Memorial Hall was opened by the Archbishop of Dublin in October 1941, and has proved a valuable focus of Parish and community life to this day.

With the development of a venue for social activities, Parish life around St Thomas's developed apace. A second curate was employed, to reside in Mount Merrion and to devote his time and energy to that end of the Parish. The affairs of the church were managed by a local church committee, consisting of the three clergymen, nine others (all men at that time), one people's church warden and one rector's church warden, and they were directly responsible to the Select Vestry of Taney Parish. Three Sunday services were held, at 10.15am, 11.30am and 7.15pm, and Intercession Service on Thursdays at 8.15pm. A children's service was held on the first Sunday in each month, and Sunday School in the Monk Gibbon Hall on the other Sundays.

By 1944, the hall was also home to meetings of the Table Tennis Club ('large membership'), the Badminton club ('full membership'), the Debating Society ('most popular, good membership, well supported'), as well as the Brownies, choir practice, a sale of work, and a youth conference. The Parish report, referring to this last, remarked: 'that there is a very real danger to our Church and to Protestantism in this part of the country cannot be denied, and a great many of our people need the stirring influence of conferences and such like, to make them realise their responsibilities, if our old Church of Ireland is to be preserved'. Similar feelings were expressed in relation to the Sunday School: 'The importance of all children in the neighbourhood attending the Sunday School regularly cannot be too strongly emphasised, especially in these difficult times.'

Despite such concerns, St Thomas's continued to flourish. The St Thomas's branch of the Mothers' Union, for example, was started in 1947, while membership of the Sunday School and other Parish organisations continued to grow. The 1946 report commented that, 'A feature of St. Thomas' Church, which unfortunately is not common to Protestant Churches in most parts of Éire, is the comparatively large congregations attending the two Sunday Morning Services; on Special Feast Days the capacity of the building is strained almost beyond its limit.'

In 1951, the Monk Gibbon Hall was extended to give additional accommodation to the caretaker and to provide a committee room, paid for with the help of a loan from the Representative Church Body. A further loan was obtained for the purpose of building a clergyman's residence adjacent to the church, despite the fact that the house was not, strictly speaking, a glebe within the meaning of the Church of Ireland Constitution. This house was completed in April 1953.

Clearly, the scene was being set for the separation of St Thomas's from Taney Parish. By now, there were 375 Church of Ireland families, and 900 individuals, within the catchment area. Negotiations took place as to geographical boundary divisions and division of financial resources. The Register of Vestrymen was divided proportionately. At the Easter Vestry in April 1956, the rector, Canon A.W.F. Orr, expressed his sorrow at the breaching of the tie between the two parts of the Parish, and, in the next month, final permission for the separation was received from the Representative Church Body. On 22 June 1956, the Reverend Trevor Hipwell was nominated to the incumbency, and after almost 100 years, the Chapel of Ease of Taney Parish became a Parish church in its own right, the Parish church of St Thomas's Mount Merrion.

CHAPTER 8

GLEBELANDS AND GLEBEHOUSES

In the nineteenth century, the glebelands stretched from the site of the previous rectory, built in 1869 (where Old Rectory Park is now), across to the graveyard, unbroken apart from the road through to Windy Arbour. Gradually over the past 150 years, parts of this property have been sold off, not always with enthusiasm. The Dublin and Dundrum Railway Company, for example, exercised its right of compulsory purchase, paying almost £900 to run the railway through the middle of the site. Following the passing of Gladstone's Irish Church Act in 1869, further portions passed to the occupying tenants, leaving the graveyard and adjoining field and the still extensive gardens attached to the glebehouse.

The Representative Church Body library contains a considerable collection of documents pertaining to the sale and purchase of church property. One such is the 'Conveyance of Addition to churchyard for Dublin Central Asylum', dated 27 March 1869, when seven perches of land were added. (A perch was 30¼ square yards, one fortieth of a rood. A rood was one quarter of an acre.) Another is a map of Taney glebe, drawn up around 1871, showing the railway. It reveals the site of the glebelands at that time as being six acres, three roods and twelve perches in total, less two roods for the road intersection.

In 1903, the Select Vestry came up with a money-making idea, involving the use of the land adjoining the graveyard (then let out for farming at £4-10-0d a year) to build cottages on. This was not, however, proceeded with. In 1913, a small portion adjoining the graveyard was conveyed to Rathdown Rural District Council, for the purpose of building a Carnegie Library. The frontage of the library site was seventy-three feet, while the back-to-front width was eighty-five feet. The price was £100, and the legal fees for both parties were met by the purchasers. This library provides a valuable amenity in Dundrum to this day.

The acreage was actually increased in 1923, when the Select Vestry decided to purchase two acres adjoining the glebe from the then rector, William Monk Gibbon. For this they obtained a loan of £350 from the Representative Church Body, at £5-7-2d per cent per annum, repayable over thirty-five years. Monk Gibbon had acquired this plot for £300 from the Earl of Pembroke, and a further £50 had been required for fencing. The primary reason for the purchase had been to prevent a housing development, for, as Acting Honorary Secretary of the Select Vestry L.S. Smith wrote

Walls and trees have to give way to traffic – Taney Road widening works.

in his loan application, 'since his purchase, the remaining land has been acquired and built on by the late Government in the interests of demobilised soldiers. It is solely due to the purchase of these two acres that homes have not been built close up against the Rectory, and the walk of the Glebe Avenue.'

The report of the Quinquennial Commission, who inspected the glebe in November 1926, notes that the acreage was now seven acres, two roods and twelve perches. Six acres were under grass, and the remainder in garden and shrubbery. The tenement value of the house was £60, that of the lands was £14, and the whole is described as being in good order.

In January 1937, Letitia Overend wrote to the Diocesan Council on behalf of the Select Vestry, referring to the above-mentioned two acres, for which the Parish still owed £278. She requested permission for one of the acres to be sold, to provide some financial liquidity. In April 1937, the Representative Body consented 'to the leasing of one acre of Glebeland at Taney, comprised in the Conveyance dated 20 December 1923, to Mr William Sweetman for the sum of £185. The lease … is to run forever at a rent of £1 per annum and is to provide that one house may be erected on the ground …'

In June 1938, permission was sought from the Diocesan Glebe Committee 'to erect a strictly temporary structure on one of the Glebe fields here. It is intended to act as a pavilion for our Parish Lawn Tennis Club. The proposed building would have no permanent foundation.' The Tennis Club continues to flourish in the same site today, and is now celebrating eighty successful years. When the Taney Village houses and lands were sold in 2013, negotiations with the builder who bought them ensured that the Tennis Club, in addition to its old right-of-way, was given a full new entrance. This access would be of use should the Parish decide to develop the tennis courts site in the future. The tennis courts were also refurbished, and the ground around them tidied up.

The year 1945 saw the conveyance of a quarter-acre behind the library to the Rathdown Board of Assistance for the building of a new dispensary and Child Welfare clinic, referred to today as the Health Centre. This followed discussions and negotiations over a period of three years. The Select Vestry set out a list of strict conditions attached to the sale of the property. This included a stipulation that the building should be no higher than twenty-five feet, that no building other than the dispensary and necessary out-offices should be erected, and that noise levels should be restricted. The County Council's valuers suggested a price of £30, fee simple, but the Vestry held out for £50 and this was achieved. In 1970, the Parish received a further £20 compensation, when the County Council took over a portion of the clinic's grounds.

Also in 1945, the County Council purchased a small portion of land on the south side of St Nahi's for road-widening. This is at the lower end of the Upper Churchtown Road side of the graveyard, to the right as one enters the gate. The Parish has a copy of the indenture paper from this transaction. The Parish would now like to buy this little piece of land for use as columbarium/garden of remembrance to supplement the one beside the church. Negotiations are ongoing and dependent on permission being granted for the burial of ashes there.

The next major development was to be the leasing of a plot of ground adjacent to St Nahi's Churchyard for the building of a bungalow. Agreement to a lease for a term of 999 years, at a yearly rent of £5 and subject to a fine of £25, was given by the Representative Body in December 1947, and a bungalow was erected on the site with an acreage of two roods and twenty-four perches. Another half-acre was sold in 1950 to one George Doyle for £700. It had a frontage on to the main Dundrum Road, and was developed as a shopping area. The year 1961 saw the loss of a patch of ground, six perches and eleven square yards, from the front of Christ Church Taney, for the purpose of road widening, while in 1972 a further £1,500 was received in compensation for land lost to road widening on the other side of Taney Road.

In 1984, Altamont Hall on Stoney Road was put up for sale, and the Parish considered buying it. It was freehold, on two acres, and would have extended the church grounds, allowing the Parish to build a new rectory and four new tennis courts, as well as to alter and extend the house on the site for use as a Parish centre. It went for auction on 8 May 1985, but Taney representatives who attended felt the bidding went too high, and Taney did not buy it.

During the process of planning for the new Parish Centre during the 1980s, legal difficulties arose regarding the land that was to be the site of the new centre. It emerged that the plot on which the old parochial hall was situated, and that to the east of the Parish church, were held on lease, and not owned outright by the Church.

The Eglinton Terrace site had been leased by the Earl of Pembroke to the Representative Body by a lease dated 16 November 1878, to hold for 150 years from 25 March of that year, at 1/- per year. The plot alongside the church had been leased from the Earl of Pembroke for 150 years from the same date, again at 1/- per year. This lease contained a covenant by the lessees that no buildings were to be erected and no burials made on the plot without permission of the lessor, and that the grounds and entrance gates thereto were to be kept in good order. The plot of ground in question measured one acre, two roods and two perches. The rent was to be paid half-yearly, and if unpaid, repossession could take place. In 1989, the Parish was able to buy out these leases from Pembroke Estates for £5,000, thus permitting the sale of the parochial hall and the building of the Parish Centre.

On 27 June 1996, Dun Laoghaire–Rathdown County Council wrote to the Parish, enclosing a map and giving notice of the making of a compulsory purchase order, under Section 76 of the third schedule of the Housing Act 1966, for a small piece of land (0.01 hectares) below the graveyard. This was to provide for the Dundrum Bypass. The compensation paid when the purchase went ahead in 2003 was €1,250 plus the legal costs of the RCB.

The first rector of Taney, Andrew Noble Bredin, was appointed in 1851, and the annual valuation of the rectory in that year, as appeared in the Books and Records of the Ecclesiastical Commissioners for Ireland, amounted to £294-17-6d. We know little detail about the residence of Reverend Bredin, but when Alfred Hamilton succeeded to the incumbency in 1867, he found himself paying £80 rent per annum, and he felt that a new glebehouse should be built on the glebelands.

Frederick Darley was appointed architect, and Thomas Holbrook of Great Brunswick Street the builder. The final cost was £1,286-15-6d, paid in part from the £884-13-10d that the Railway Company had earlier paid to the Parish and that had been invested in 3% Government Stock, the rector agreeing to forgo the income he had been receiving from this investment. The remainder of £700 was raised by subscription following an appeal to parishioners. The architectural drawings, bills of quantity and other documentation concerning the rectory can be inspected in the Representative Church Body library. It was a large, detached house with lawns.

Francis Elrington Ball and Everard Hamilton tell us, in their Taney Parish history of 1895, that in 1974, the Parish borrowed £200 from the Board of Works to build a stable. The loan was payable in thirty-five annual instalments of £10-8-0d. The rector of the time, Reverend Alfred Hamilton, paid rent to the Parish for the house, in part payment of annual payments required to provide for the stipends of future clergy. However, the next rector would not have to pay rent on the Glebe House.

In the 1950s, it was felt that this house was very old-fashioned and consideration was given to selling it. However, nothing came of this, and the idea was allowed to lapse for the time being. The matter was raised again in the 1970s, and a sub-committee was set up to consider the options. Pembroke Estates were approached, and they replied that they would have no objection in principle to the building of a new rectory on the church grounds. At the Select Vestry meeting of 3 February 1978, however, a proposal that the Vestry apply for outline planning permission to build a rectory on the church grounds was defeated by six votes to five, with three abstentions. A possible house in Sydenham Villas came on the market, but was rejected as too old and not suitable for families with children.

Then, at the meeting of the Select Vestry on 13 February 1979, the Chairman, Canon W.J.M. Burrows, brought to the notice of the meeting that number 6 Stoney Road was about to come on the market. This was considered very suitable, being situated alongside the church. The Representative Church Body gave its approval, and a bridging loan, and in April 1979, the house was purchased for the Parish at a cost of £69,500, with majority, though not unanimous, approval of the Select Vestry. At auction the following October, the old house and grounds raised £215,000 and the coach house mews £15,000.

At the General Easter Vestry of April 1980, the Parish treasurer, Tim Keatinge, gave the following details of the transactions:

Receipts from sale of Old Rectory and Mews	£230,000
Purchase of new Rectory, including fees, interest	£79,000
Estimate to complete decoration of new Rectory	£12,000
Selling expenses, including advertising	£9,800
Other	£1,800

£120,000 of the resulting surplus capital was placed on three-month deposit, earning eighteen percent interest. The balance of £7,400 remained on deposit with the Representative Body. The old rectory was ultimately demolished, and the lands used for a housing development named Old Rectory Park.

At the same Easter Vestry, the rector reported that he and his family were very pleased with the house, and particularly with the location. Towards the end of the 1980s, nevertheless, it was felt that the new rectory required upgrading and extending, to provide more privacy for the rector and his family. Work on this was carried out during 1992–93, being paid for not out of parochial funds, but from part of the surplus from the sale of the sold glebe, which had been vested in the Representative Church Body.

In 2011–12, a major refurbishment programme was carried out to upgrade the rectory before the arrival of Canon Robert Warren. This involved rewiring, provision of good insulation, installation of a new boiler, fitting of solar heating panels, improvement of the plumbing, realignment to provide a study, and full modernisation and decoration. The house now performs well its dual functions of a modern, comfortable home for the rector and his family and a place of Parish business.

As is explained in the chapter on the planned Taney Village development, further property was purchased at the beginning of the twenty-first century, but was sold again. The current Glebelands consist of Christ Church Taney, its grounds and buildings, the rectory at 6 Stoney Road, St Nahi's Church and its large graveyard, and the tennis courts.

Every ten years, the RCB requires an inspection of Parish buildings, to detect faults before they become too serious or expensive. Included must be a specialised inspection for rot, woodworm and other infestations. Acceptable inspectors include chartered building surveyors, chartered engineers and qualified architects. The work must be carried out in a professional capacity, with professional indemnity insurance; it cannot be done for free by parishioners. In Taney's case, inspections take place in the middle of each decade. However, the ongoing oversight of maintenance and repairs lies with the Select Vestry and glebewardens, and this is carried out in an exemplary manner by the current incumbents.

Chapter 9

Rectors and Curates

The benefice of Taney was part of the Archdeaconry of Dublin from the thirteenth century until 1851, when, on the death of Archdeacon Torrens, it became a separate parish. The J.B. Leslie papers, lodged in the library of the Representative Church Body in Dublin, list the curates who served under the archdeacon of Dublin prior to 1851, and the rectors and curates who have served thereafter. The earliest reference is to Matthew, 'Dean of Taney' around 1235. A further note mentions that 'In 1547 the Rectory or prebend was leased to Richard Rede, Knight, he to find a Chaplain for Taney.'

The following is the list of curates who ministered under the Archdeacon of Dublin, as nominated in Leslie's succession list:

1615	Robert Pont is C. Taney, Rathfarnham and Donnybrook (R.V.) V. Rathdrum 16 July 1918
1630	Richard Prescott C. of the same. T.C.D.B.A. 1620, M.A. 1623
1639–40	Thomas Naylor is C. became V. Kildroght 1640
1679	John Sankey Lic. 8 May to Rathfarnham, Donnybrook, Kilgobbin, Taney, Cruagh and Whitechurch
1753	Mervy Archdall – Lic. P.C. 2 Oct, also to Kilgobbin
1758	Jeremy Walsh – Lic. 1 September at £35 and Book Money. P.C. Taney 1758–87. Was also P.C. Kilgobbin

1787	William Dwyer – Lic. 10 January at £50
1787	Matthew Campbell – Lic. 9 November at £50. Became P.C. Kilgobbin 1813, was P.C. Taney 1787–1813
1814	Richard Ryan – Lic. 15 April. P.C. Taney 1814–20. V. Rathconnell from 1820
1820	Henry Hunt – Lic. 21 July. Seems to have exchanged with Ryan, who went to Rathconnell, County Meath, 1820. P.C. Taney 1820–21
1821	William Ford Vance – Res. 1821
1821	James Bulwer – Res. 1824 for Booterstown
1824	Henry Hamilton – P.C. Taney 1824–25
1825	Alexander Burrowes Campbell – Nominated 23 August 1825; Lic. 24 February, P.C. Taney 1825–28
1830	James Prior – Lic P.C. 8 March P.C. Taney 1830–34
1834	Samuel Henry Mason (died 1863 by falling overboard from the Mail Steamer near Holyhead) – C. Taney 1834–36
1836	Clement Archer Schoales – C. Taney 1836–37
1837	William Henry Stanford – C. Taney 1836-37. P.C. 1837–51

In 1851, the Parish was severed from the Archdeaconry and became a rectory. Our rectors were:

1851	Andrew Nobel Bredin. Inst. 1 August. Res 1857 for Preb. Dunlavin
1857	Edward Busteed Moeran. Res. 1867 for R. Killyleagh, County Down
1867	William Alfred Hamilton – died 1895
1895	John Joseph Robinson – Res. 1901
1901	William Monk Gibbon – died March 1935
1935	Adrian William Fielder Orr
1959	Walter Joseph Mayes Burrows. Inst. 6 March
1983	William Desmond Sinnamon
2012	Robert Warren

The last eight rectors of Taney.
Top row (left to right): Canon Robert Warren, Canon William Desmond Sinnamon, Canon Walter J. M. Burrows.
Middle row (left to right): Canon W.F. Orr, Canon William Monk Gibbon, Rev. John Joseph Robinson.
Far left: Rev. William Alfred Hamilton.
Left: Rev. Edward Busteed Moeran.

Our curates, nowadays known as 'curate assistants', were:

1822	William Ford (res. C.)
1836–37	William Henry Stanford
1844	William Fitzpatrick
1852–55	John Joseph Knox Fletcher
1855–56	Charles Seymour Langley
1857–58	Robert William Whelan
1858–60	John Fawcett
1860–61	James Hornidge Walsh
1862–65	John Hobart Seymour
1866–68	Robert Baker Stoney
1868–90	Edward Arnold Carroll
1890–91	John Edward Murray
1892–93	Ralph Walker
1893–95	James William Ffranck Sheppard
1896–99	Herbert McVittie Taylor
1901–02	Thomas Dagg
1902–10	William McClelland Kerr
1910–13	William Luxmore Jameson
1913–21	Ernest Maunsell Bateman
1921–24	Arthur Theodore Irvine Fod
1925–28	George John Foxter Verschoyle
1928–29	Norman William Brabazon Gifford Harvey
1930–32	Victor Joseph Pike
1932–37	St John Surridge Pike
1937	George Douglas Hobson
1941	Victor Thomas McClaughry
1943	John Coote Duggan
1947	Edmund Gibson Shearer
1948	Robert George McCollum
1949	Trevor Senior Hipwell (May 1951 to Monkstown, returned to Taney in November 1951 owing to difficulty finding a curate assistant for this larger parish)

From here, the description 'curate' is changed to 'curate assistant' in the later notes added to Leslie's list:

1955	Brian Haddon Campion
1958	Richard Groves Large
1963	Frederick Charles Young
1967	Robert Desmond Harmon
1970	Arthur Horace Nelson McKinley
1976	Robin Edward Bantry White
1979	William John Rowland Crawford Also Slator, E.D.H., part-time C. Taney (1974–80)
1984	David George Harwood Frazer
1987	Robert Chase Reed
1988	David George Moynan
1990	Frederick Charles Appelbe
1992	Bruce Andrew Pierce
1993	Nigel Kenneth Dunne
1994	Peter Robert Campion
1997	Ivan Moore
1997	Bernadette Theresa Daly
2000	Jonathan Douglas Pierce
2000	Ronald Horace Watts
2001	Sonya Giles
2003	Leonard John Tanner
2005	Bernadette Theresa Daly
2007	Niall James Sloane
2008	Stephen Andrew Farrell
2011–12	Bernadette Theresa Daly (Priest in Charge)
2013	John (Jack) Alfred Harold Kinkead
2015	Catherine Jane Hallissey
2016	Nigel Pierpoint

Taney Parish has, at various times, benefitted from the services of second curate assistants. This has been particularly helpful since the 1990s, when the size and population of the Parish and the complexity of the work involved has required the provision, whenever possible, of a clerical team of rector and two curates. Thus the tenure of many of the more recent curates has overlapped with that of a colleague.

It should be noted that in the hiatus between the retirement of Canon Desmond Sinnamon at the end of September 2011 and the installation of Canon Robert Warren in September 2012, our former curate, Reverend Bernadette Daly, generously stepped in to serve for one year as Priest in Charge, and did a sterling job of running the Parish.

At present, our team comprises our rector, Robert, and our two curate assistants, Cathy and Nigel (all affectionately known in the Parish by their Christian names). These three talented people work successfully to blend together their spiritual, pastoral, administrative and social skills to the benefit of Taney parishioners of all ages.

CHAPTER 10

TANEY AS A PLACE OF WORSHIP AND NURTURE

A parish is not merely a geographical unit with a church as its centrepiece; it is a community of people belonging and associating on diverse levels, with worship and prayer in the church as a focus. Meeting for worship is not only the primary function of a parish, but also the initial contact for most people. Sharing in worship and prayer both initiates and consolidates the sense of fellowship between parishioners and deepens friendships between them.

At each Sunday service, the number attending (usually 200 to 300 at the main 10.15am service nowadays, and many more on special feast days) is recorded in the Preachers' Book, along with the number of communicants; people are counted by the church wardens as they enter the church. The name of the person preaching the sermon, cash collected and collections for special causes are also noted and the book is signed by the preacher. Lenten lunches are held once a week in the Parish Centre during Lent, and the money raised is donated to charities operating in developing countries.

The Preachers' Book of 1912 tells of a special collection of £9-15-0d towards the Titanic Disaster Fund. Charity collections are a frequent feature, including collections for the Jews Society,

Above: Taney choir celebration.

Below: Christ Church Taney on a busy morning, 1990s.

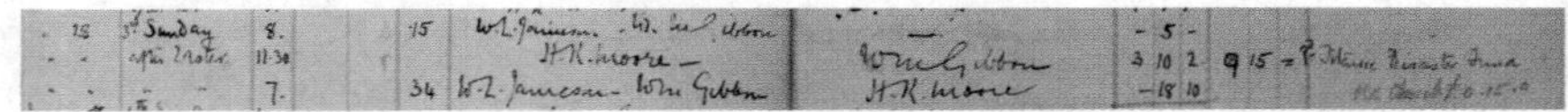

The Preachers' Book of 1912: £9-15-0d was donated to the Titanic Disaster Fund

Orange Societies, the Red Cross during the First World War and Dundrum Prisoners of War in August 1918. Today they might include a collection for Christian Aid, or for a relief fund set up to assist after a major disaster such as a tsunami, earthquake or famine.

The schedule of services has changed slightly over the years. We know from the 1961 Select Vestry Report (published in 1962) that the early Sunday services in Christ Church on the second, fourth and fifth Sundays of the month were held at 8am at that time. The main services, whether Holy Communion on the first and third Sundays or Morning Prayer on second, fourth and fifth Sundays, were at 11.30, with Evening Prayer at 7pm. Sunday School began at 10.10am in the Parochial Hall, and there was an additional Parents' and Children's Service on the second Sunday at 10.30am. There was Morning Prayer at 10am on weekdays, and Holy Communion at 10.30am on Wednesday mornings.

At St Nahi's church, there was a Holy Communion service at 8am on the first and third Sundays, and an Evening Prayer service on Wednesdays at 8pm. The main service, Morning Prayer most weeks with Holy Communion and hymns on the fourth Sunday, was held at 10.15am.

Both churches were then open daily for prayer and meditation from 8am to 8pm. The report notes that 'All seats in St. Nahi's are free. Seats in Christ Church are allocated if desired, but all seats are free at commencement of Service.'

A service was held at the Central Mental Hospital in Dundrum each Sunday at 9.30am, with Holy Communion on each second Sunday. Today, insufficient demand means that there is now no regular service there. The rector celebrates Holy Communion at the hospital at times such as Christmas and Easter, when a patient requests this.

Enjoying a cup of coffee after Wednesday morning service.

Today, the Sunday services at St Nahi's Church are held at 8.30am and 11.45am. Christ Church has its main service at 10.15am, followed by refreshments in the Parish Centre, and an evening one at 7pm. There is still a service, usually Holy Communion, on Wednesdays at 10am, when prayers are said, with names given, for parishioners now living in nursing homes, for those are ill and for those who are bereaved. This service is also followed by coffee and tea in the centre, giving another opportunity for socialising in the Parish context. The Taney Bible Study and Prayer Group continues to meet once a month in the Parish Centre.

Sunday School is now held at 10.15am, while the church service is on, as is a crèche for younger children, except on the second Sunday of the month, when there is a Family Service. Around once a month, there is a Sunday evening Youth Service, with food and refreshments afterwards.

Worship in Taney is beautifully enhanced by superb organ playing and a top-class choir in each church, the Taney Occasional Chorus and a lovely children's choir who sing the blessing at baptisms. The Taney Youth Band makes a great contribution too at occasional services.

Clockwise from top left: Christian Aid service; Santa visits the Christmas Bazaar; a chat in the coffee shop; the Junior Choir rehearsing; Taney School Orchestra perform at the Christmas Bazaar; members of Taney playschool enjoying their morning's work; and a lively discussion at Sunday School.

Taney uses a combination of prayer books and service sheets for its services, the old hymn books being rather unwieldy for some parishioners to hold. In 2004, the Church of Ireland launched a new prayer book and, on 21 April 2004, an order was placed for twenty-five boxes of pew edition prayer books, twelve copies of the desk edition and twenty copies of the large print edition, at a cost of €2,358. These are handed out by the churchwardens at the beginning of the services, and tidied up by them afterwards. Today, we have short forms in our churches for newcomers to the Parish to fill in. New parishioners can inform the Parish Office of contact details, so that they can be introduced to the Parish and its activities.

The churches host baptisms, confirmations, weddings and funerals; being a lively, busy parish, there are many. From June 1967 to January 2005, there were 977 baptisms. From 2005 to 2017, 416 children were baptised, a very healthy number. From August 2002 to April 2007, forty-nine marriages were performed in Taney, and from December 2007 to October 2016, there were fifty-eight marriages.

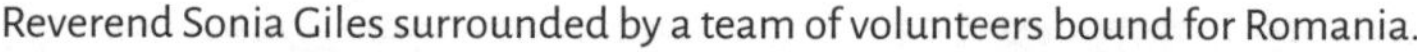

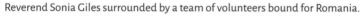

Reverend Sonia Giles surrounded by a team of volunteers bound for Romania.

Between November 1950 and October 2016, 766 funerals were registered. In 2017, twenty-eight young people were confirmed in Christ Church Taney by the Archbishop of Dublin, His Grace the Most Reverend Michael Jackson – twenty-six parishioners, one candidate from Wesley College and one from Kilternan Parish.

Special services take place during Lent, at Easter, at Harvest Festival and at Christmas. The 'Christmas Carols by Candlelight' service is very popular, as is the midnight service on Christmas Eve. The services marking the institutions of, and farewells to, rectors always fill the churches to capacity. There are close ties with Taney Parish Primary School, with the schoolchildren attending a church service several times a year.

The Taney Care Group was set up on 5 September 1985, to assist parishioners of older age or with mobility difficulties to come, or be brought, to church for main church festivals, for their own Holy Communion or for Songs of Praise service, followed by an enjoyable social event. One such event was the St Valentine's Party in 1987,

An impressive team of volunteers preparing the church for the Harvest Festival.

The church staircase resplendent in its Harvest livery.

which included tea and snacks, a beetle drive and a sing-along. The Care Group has evolved into the Taney Friends and Social Club, and is well supported. The aim of the Club is to keep in close contact with those who find it harder to get out of their homes, and to bring old friends together in the church setting.

In the 1950s, services marking the Women's World Day of Prayer were started in St Nahi's church in the evening. These were moved to the morning in Christ Church Taney in the 1960s. Initially, they were attended by Taney parishioners and their Methodist and Presbyterian friends, but after the Second Vatican Council concluded in 1965, the Roman Catholic Church became interested and, in the late 1970s, parishioners of Holy Cross began to attend. More recently, these services have been shared with Holy Cross Church Dundrum, Dundrum Methodist Church, St Attracta's Church, Ballinteer, and St John the Evangelist Church, Ballinteer, the last one in Taney being a service written by Egyptian women in 2013. These interdenominational services take place in an international context, providing a prayer link with women across the globe, while also bringing local women together for worship and fellowship.

The Armenian Church in Ireland holds its services and Sunday School in Christ Church Taney on Sundays, led by Dr Paul Manook, and they have shared services and hospitality with Taney parishioners, developing friendships and understanding between the communities. Taney Parish shared in the centenary commemorations for the Armenian genocide, and supported the erection of the Khackbar memorial in the grounds of Christchurch Cathedral.

A special service was held on Friday, 14 September 2001, 'A Service of Prayer for Healing and Peace in our World remembering all those who have been touched by the tragic events in the USA'. This was to commemorate those killed and injured in the attack by Islamic terrorist group Al Qaeda on what is known as '9/11', 11 September 2001. On that day, almost 3,000 people were killed and over 6,000 injured when four aeroplanes were hijacked and flown deliberately into buildings – two into the 'twin towers' of the World Trade Centre in Manhattan, one into the Pentagon in Washington and one that crashed in Pennsylvania. Amid the world's shock, people of faith all over the planet came together to pray. The Taney community was part of that movement of solidarity.

During the 'Troubles' in Northern Ireland, many parishes forged links with their counterparts in the north. Taney partnered with Ballyholme Parish, near Bangor in County Down. On 19 November 1994, three Taney parishioners – Alan Hamilton, Dudley Dolan and Carol Robinson Tweed – travelled to the Ballymascanlon House Hotel in Dundalk, meeting Maia Taylor and Michael Arlow from Ballyholme to cement this relationship and set plans in motion for future liaison. While this contact has now faded, a new contact was developed in 2014 with Omey Parish in Connemara, County Galway, and exchange visits have taken place.

In 2018, Taney has the good fortune to be served by a dedicated, hard-working, flexible and cheerful team of clergy – the rector, Canon Robert Warren, and two curate assistants, Reverend Cathy Hallisey and Reverend Nigel Pierpoint, and assistant priest Reverend Bernie Daly – as well as two lay readers, Trilly Keatinge and Fionnuala Drury.

Parishioners help to serve Holy Communion wine, lead the Prayers of the People and read some of the lessons. Parishioners are involved in serving as churchwardens, and there is now a small panel of assistant churchwardens, who serve one Sunday a month and on special occasions, and take the collection. Others polish the brass and silver, launder the Communion linen and, as members of the Chancel Guild, decorate the church with flowers. There is a sense that everyone is a part of what is going on in church.

In 2016, Taney sadly had fifteen deaths in the Parish and five other families or individuals moved away, but the good news was that twenty-five new families joined the Parish. Attendances at church remain good and a recent Parish survey indicated that people are in general very happy with how services are conducted. It is encouraging that the Parish is flourishing as we celebrate the bicentenary of Christ Church Taney.

CHAPTER 11

RUNNING A LARGE PARISH – ADMINISTRATION AND FINANCES

Pre-Disestablishment

When the extant records of Taney begin, 227 years ago, the Church of Ireland was the church established by law in this country, and it held a privileged position. It was the church of only a small minority of the population, yet it was the State church. It was well endowed, and supported through tithes by the entire population. Tithes were originally paid in kind (in produce), but, following the Tithe Composition Act of 1832, payment was made in money. Tithes were computed at one-tenth of annual income, and were a tax on the occupiers of land. Tenants had to pay, regardless of the church to which they belonged.

Roman Catholics and Dissenters resented these payments, and following discontent throughout the county during the 1830s, the Tithe Computation Act of 1838 converted the tithe into a rent charge on the land, payable not by the tenant, but by the landlord.

This was calculated at seventy-five percent of the value of the tithes. Although many landlords passed the new tithe rent charge on to their tenants in the form of rent increases, grievances were reduced, as the tax now became an indirect one.

The Taney tithes were paid to the Archdeacon of Dublin, who then paid the curate's stipend. At a special Vestry meeting held on 13 November 1824, £450 sterling was confirmed as the amount 'due and payable to the Venerable John Torrens, Archdeacon of Dublin, as a composition for the tithe claimable by him, as Ecclesiastical Incumbent of the said Parish of Taney, said sum of £450 sterling having been agreed to by the said Incumbent, with the assent in writing of His Grace the Lord Archbishop of Dublin as Bishop of the Diocese and patron of the Benefice'. When, in 1851, the Archdeacon ceased to act as rector and Taney was given its own rector, the tithe rent charges were paid directly to him, and he then paid the curate. Subsequently, the Parish took responsibility for paying the curate by the raising of voluntary subscriptions.

(7)

Dr. The Accompt of Edward Mayne & Stepn Stock ending Easter Tuesday April 2d 1793

	£	s	d
To balance handed over by the former Church Wardens	..	19	8¼
To the amount of one years applotment on said Parish	33	18	11½
	34	18	7¾
To Balance due to Church Wardens	...	14	11½

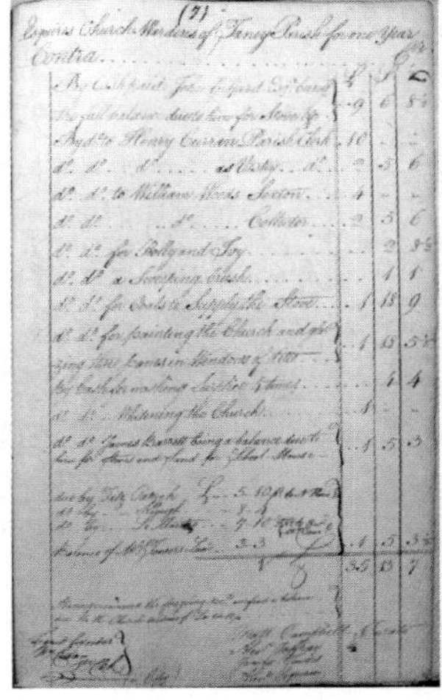

Above: A page from the Parish Applotment Book, 1793, showing accounts prepared by Edward Mayne.
Right: A sample of Taney Parish accounts, showing expenses for the year ending Easter Tuesday, 22 April 1794, taken from the Vestry Minute Book of that year.

Expenditure for the year ending Easter Tuesday, 22 April 1794 (taken from the Vestry Minutes for that year):

By Henry Curran his salary as Parish Clerk	£10.0.0
By Henry Curran his salary as Vestry Clerk	£2.5.6
By William Woods his salary as Sexton	£4.11.0
By William Woods his salary as Collector	£2.5.6
By cash for coals to supply stove	£1.0.6
By cash for holly and ivy for the Church	£0.2.8½
By cash for washing the surplice 4 times	£0.4.4
By cash for a sweeping brush	£0.1.3
By cash for pointing the roof of the Church	£3.0.0
By cash due by the Parish to the Charity School	£7.0.2½
By cash for a coffin for Mary Byrne's child	£0.3.3
By cash for a coffin for Catherine Mulligan	£0.6.6
By cash for the bell rope	£0.1.7½
By cash overcharged Lord Trimbleston 28 acres at 31/2d	£0.8.2
By arrears due by Mr Tower's land or Tenants of the former year	£0.3.3
By arrears due by Edward Keough's land or Tenants of the former year	£0.8.4
Arrears of 1793 due by Edward Keogh paid	£0.4.4½
Arrears for Isaac Simmond's land or Tenants of the former year	£0.3.2½
Arrears due by Honourable Tankerville Chamberlaine's Land or Tenants of the former year (paid)	£0.2.4
Arrears due by James Kavanagh's land or Tenants of the former year (paid)	£0.0.10½
Arrears due by Michael Reilly's land or tenants of the former year	£0.14.7
By balance remaining in the hands of Judge Chamberlaine and A. Jaffray Esquire to be handed over to the new Church Wardens Jas. Potts and J.L. Hume Esq	£2.18.1½
	£36.5.7½

Further sources of income included marriage and burial fees, which were paid directly to the curate and, after 1851, to the rector, as well as offertories and special collections held for the schools, the poor, and so forth. There was also the Parish cess, levied on land holders to provide for the maintenance and general running of the church and the payment of Parish officers. The early Vestry minute books provide excellent records of the land holders, the acreages they held, and the amount of cess paid by each. The cess applottment rate for the year ending Easter Tuesday, 7 April 1795, for instance, was 3½d per acre.

To administer the cess applottment scheme, until 1821 Taney Parish appointed two 'appraisers', who made the valuations on which assessment was based. Until 1862, after which the church cess ceased to be levied, two or three 'applotters' were appointed each year to applot the assessments on the parishioners. On 24 June 1794, for example, the Vestry appointed Francis Marchant, Leonard Ely and James Towers applotters of the church cess for the following year, while the previous year's appraisers, Alexander Pakenham and James Barrett, were reappointed. So, too, was the 'parish constable', William Stammers. His was an unpaid appointment until 1806, when, according to the Parish accounts of that year, Michael Gould was paid a salary of £2-5-6d to act as constable for the year.

A 'beadle' was also appointed on an annual basis; in 1802, he was paid £2-5-6d for his services for the year. In 1829, the posts of Parish Constable and Beadle, both of whom were engaged in law enforcement, were amalgamated, and in 1862, the office was abolished.

The Parish employed 'collectors of cess', who were paid an annual salary and a bonus related to their efficiency. In 1861, William Woods received £6-16-6d as collector, plus a further £1-2-9d for 'Industry in collecting the Parish Cesses' in addition to £4-11-0d in his capacity as sexton. After 1832, payment to the sexton, like that to the Parish clerk, was paid by the Ecclesiastical Commissioners. The position of Parish clerk and of vestry clerk were, in the early part of the nineteenth century, held by the same person. In 1801, Henry Curran earned £10-0-0d as Parish clerk, and £6-16-6d as vestry clerk. The duties of the vestry clerk are laid out in the minutes of the Easter Vestry of 1836 as follows:

To receive instructions from Clergymen and Church Wardens for serving Notices of Vestries, to prepare same and have them served by Beadle of the Parish – to upkeep the Minutes of the Vestry and to write out copies of applottments of Parish and Grand Jury Cess. Of the Grand Jury Cess there should be two copies of the applottment.

All of these positions were held by men. In 1862, the office of vestry clerk ceased to exist. Meanwhile, in 1833, the Ecclesiastical Commissioners had undertaken the payment of the expenses involved in running the church services, as well as those for repairing the church itself. After 1862, the cess for payment of the Parish officers ceased to be levied, and from that year all expenses, apart from those paid by the Ecclesiastical Commissioners, were met by voluntary subscription.

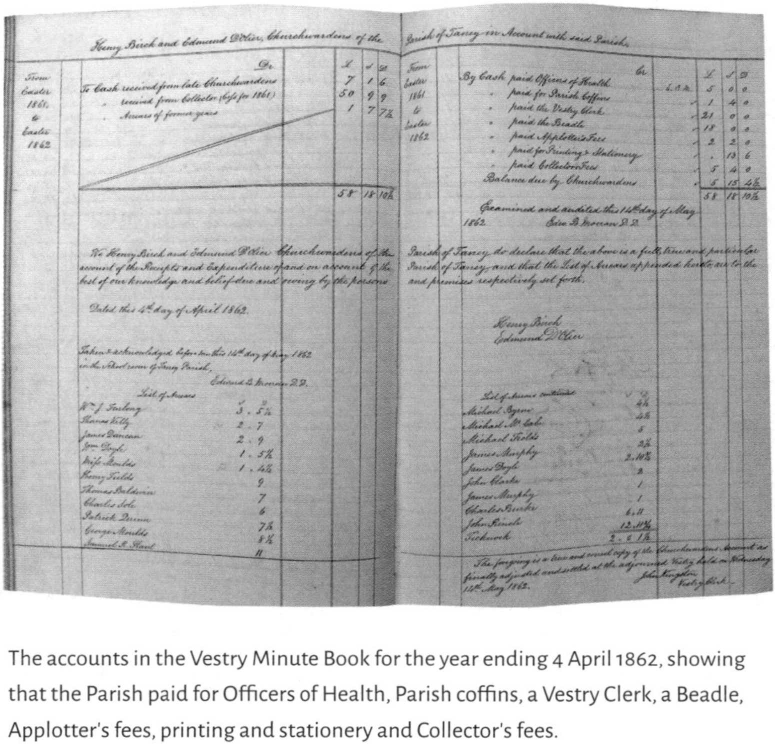

Henry Birch and Edmund D'Olier, Churchwardens of the Parish of Taney in Account with said Parish.

From Easter 1861 to Easter 1862

Dr	£	s	d
To Cash received from late Churchwardens	7	1	6
received from Collector (Cess for 1861)	50	9	9
Arrears of former years	1	7	7½
	58	18	10½

From Easter 1861 to Easter 1862

Cr	£	s	d
By Cash paid Officers of Health	5	0	0
paid for Parish Coffins	1	4	0
paid the Vestry Clerk	21	0	0
paid the Beadle	18	0	0
paid Applotter's Fees	2	2	0
paid for Printing & Stationery		13	6
paid Collector's Fees	5	4	0
Balance due by Churchwardens	5	15	4½
	58	18	10½

Examined and audited this 14th day of May 1862 Edw. B. Moeran D.D.

We Henry Birch and Edmund D'Olier Churchwardens of the Parish of Taney do declare that the above is a full, true and particular account of the Receipts and Expenditure of and on account of the Parish of Taney and that the List of Arrears appended hereto are to the best of our knowledge and belief due and owing by the persons and premises respectively set forth.

Dated this 4th day of April 1862.

Henry Birch
Edmund D'Olier

Taken & acknowledged before me this 14th day of May 1862 in the School room of Taney Parish,
Edward B. Moeran D.D.

List of Arrears

	s	d
Wm. J. Furlong	3	5½
Thomas Kelly	2	7
James Duncan	2	9
Wm. Doyle	1	5½
Miss Moulds	1	4½
Henry Fields		9
Thomas Baldwin		7
Charles Cole		6
Patrick Quinn		7½
George Moulds		8½
Samuel H. Hunt		11

List of Arrears continued

	s	d
Michael Byrne		4½
Michael McCabe		4½
Michael Fields		5
James Murphy		2½
James Doyle	2	10½
John Clarke		2
James Murphy		1
Charles Burke		1
John Reinele	6	11
Tickwick	12	11½
	2 . 0	1½

The foregoing is a true and correct copy of the Churchwardens Account as finally adjusted and settled at the adjourned Vestry held on Wednesday 14th May 1862.
John Kingston
Vestry Clerk

The accounts in the Vestry Minute Book for the year ending 4 April 1862, showing that the Parish paid for Officers of Health, Parish coffins, a Vestry Clerk, a Beadle, Applotter's fees, printing and stationery and Collector's fees.

Naturally, the management of the Parish finances prior to disestablishment in 1869 did not always go unchallenged. There were minor quibbles, as well as the occasional more serious disagreement, concerning the monetary affairs of the Parish. For the year ending Easter Tuesday 1794, for instance, Lord Trimbleston was overcharged for twenty-eight acres at 3½d, making a refund of 8/2d necessary. Meanwhile, arrears were owed by Mr Towers, Edward Keough, Isaac Simmonds, The Honourable Tankerville Chamberlaine, James Kavanagh and Michael Reilly and their respective tenants. In 1805, the payment due by Mr Mark Moran on his forty-four acres was reduced by one quarter, in view of the fact that much of his land was made up of rock and mountain. On 9 May 1826, the Vestry resolved 'that in consequence of the great inequality in the value of land in this parish, a suitable gradation should be made in the applottment of the parish cesses'. The applottment for the year ending Easter 1831 illustrates this as follows:

> *Parish Cess – 1st Quality 1/4d, 2nd Do 1/-, 3rd Do 10d, 4th Do 7d, 5th Do 5d, 6th Do 4d, 7th Do 1d.*
> *Instalment tax – 1st Quality 1/6d, 2nd Do 1/2d, 3rd Do 10d, 4th Do 7d, 5th Do 5d, 6th Do 3¼d, 7th Do 1d.*

Nevertheless, some people were not satisfied. In 1861, a legal case was taken by a John Dane against the church wardens, concerning the proceeds of the previous Easter Vestry. The case was heard at the Kilmainham Quarter Sessions, before the Honourable Charles J. Trench, who, 'after entering fully into the law, and having regard to previous decisions made, said he felt no hesitation in pronouncing the appeal to be frivolous, and one that should not, in his opinion, ever have been lodged. The proceedings at the Vestry of the parish had been for years conducted regularly, the assessments from time to time made correct, and he had no reason to interfere with the assessments made at the last Vestry in any way. He would, therefore, dismiss the appeal with £5 costs, being the full sum he could award against the appellant.' (*Irish Times*, 20 June 1861)

Still, while the Established Church did hold an unjustifiably privileged position in Irish society, it would be fair to say that parishes did make some contributions towards the community as a whole. Taney levied a cholera cess in 1833, and it was responsible for appointing 'Overseers of Deserted Children' and for appointing and paying for 'Officers of Health'. In 1847, these last allocated a sum for the purchase of lime brushes and buckets in order to have the cabins of the poor residents in the Parish whitewashed and cleansed. The following year's accounts reveal that the officers of health were paid £20, £5 was allocated for deserted children and £4 was set aside for coffins for the poor.

The Parish provided a pound, and a pound keeper, to deal with the detention of stray animals. In 1860, part of the Parish's civic duty was fulfilled by the payment of £5 to a Patrick Doolin for cleansing the lanes and alleys of Dundrum for fifty weeks at 2/- per week. A militia cess was raised at various times – that for 1807 was at 7d per acre, for 1810 3½d per acre, while the Vestry Meeting of 8 June 1813 confirmed the 'Militia Applottment of £48-5-0d towards the Quota of this Parish for 4 men'. This meeting also confirmed provision for the maintenance of roads within the Barony of Rathdown.

On 28 October 1812, a committee was formed, to report back on 1 November on 'the expediency and best mode of establishing a Dispensary in Dundrum, to promote the comforts of the poor in that village and its vicinity'. Provision was often made to pay for coffins and burials of the poor, and to provide for orphans and deserted children. April 1812 saw a concerted effort by the Parish in this regard, when the Vestry:

> *... resolved that the loyal and peaceable conduct of our poor neighbours and fellow parishioners in this parish of Taney entitle them to our affection and utmost assistance in this time of apprehended scarcity –*

Resolved that the affluent parishioners be, and are hereby called upon, to subscribe to form a fund to furnish provisions at a moderate price, to such persons inhabiting this parish as shall stand in need thereof.

The applottment lists provide us with interesting details concerning the names of landowners and landholders, and the amounts levied. For the year ending Easter Tuesday, 7 April 1795, the total acreage held within the Parish, in ninety-seven plots, was 2,362 acres. This ranged from 337 acres held in Roebuck by Lord Trimbleston to two acres in Dundrum held by Mr J. Currin. The table given in the Origins chapter illustrates the acreages ascribed to each townland. By the year ending Easter 1862, considerable changes in the distribution of land had taken place, so that the applottment of Parish cess for the year ending Easter 1863, the last year for which such lists were made, was spread among 642 occupiers, yielding £12-2-2d.

The minutes of the next Easter Vestry, held on Easter Monday, 6 April 1863, reveal the administrative changes outlined in this chapter, in the assessments made as follows:

It was resolved that the following sums be assessed:

Viz for Officers of Health	None
Deserted Children	None
Coffins for the Poor	£1-10/=
The Vestry Clerk	None (by resolution)
The Beadle	None
Applotter's Fees	None
Printing and Stationery	None
Collector's Fees	None

Thus, movement had taken place away from compulsory payments collected by paid officials, towards a situation where the Parish's expenses were met voluntarily by its own parishioners.

Post-Disestablishment

Gladstone's Irish Church Act, passed on 26 July 1869, did not merit a mention in Taney's Vestry minutes of that year, but in providing that the union between the Church of England and the Church of Ireland be dissolved, the Act effected a change in status for the Irish Church. This had consequences for the way the Church would be run.

The 1830s had seen considerable antagonism throughout the country to the payment of tithes, and to the privileged position of the Established Church. The government, by two moderate reforming measures, stemmed this tide of opposition by Roman Catholics and Dissenters, and succeeded in maintaining the strength of the Irish Establishment for a further quarter of a century.

The first of these measures, the Irish Church Temporalities Act of 1833, rationalised the Church's organisation by abolishing ten bishoprics and redistributing church endowments more equally between the wealthier and poorer incumbencies. The second, the Tithe Commutation Act of 1838, as mentioned earlier in this chapter, transferred the burden of payment of tithes from tenant to landlord. This eased the pressure on the Irish Church. As time went on, however, Roman Catholics became increasingly vocal in their demands for denominational equality in all spheres, while many liberals in Britain felt that the maintenance of the Church of Ireland as the Established Church in Ireland was the cause of many of the country's problems, since it represented an inequitable distribution of privilege and power.

It was William Gladstone (Liberal Prime Minister 1868–74, 1880–85, 1886 and 1892–94) who introduced the Bill which severed the connection between Church and State, ended the union between the churches of England and Ireland, and provided for the setting up of a governing body for the Church of Ireland, the Representative Church Body. A commission, the Commissioners of Church Temporalities, was constituted, which could transfer to the

Representative Church Body the ownership of Church properties, as well as selling Church land to occupying tenants.

The Irish Church Act came into effect on 1 January 1871, giving the Church little time to reorganise itself administratively. A General Convention of the representatives of the clergy and laity opened in Dublin on 15 February 1870, and a new Constitution was drawn up. This provided for a hierarchy of governing bodies – the parochial Select Vestries, the Diocesan Synods and the General Synod, this last to be the governing body. The Diocesan Synods were to operate the local government of the Church, and would consist of the clergy of the parishes and two laymen for each clergyman, the lay representatives to be elected by the General Vestry of each parish.

At the annual meeting of the General Vestry, members of the Select Vestry would be elected who would be responsible, along with the incumbent, for the control of parochial funds. The Select Vestry could only be elected by registered vestrymen. The proposal to include women members of vestries was defeated by 158 votes to 108. Indeed, it was not until 1922 that the first female names (Miss L. Overend and Mrs M. Murray) appear on the list of the registered vestrymen in Taney Parish, and not until 1928 that women's names appear in any significant numbers. To this day, the registers are still called 'registers of vestrymen'.

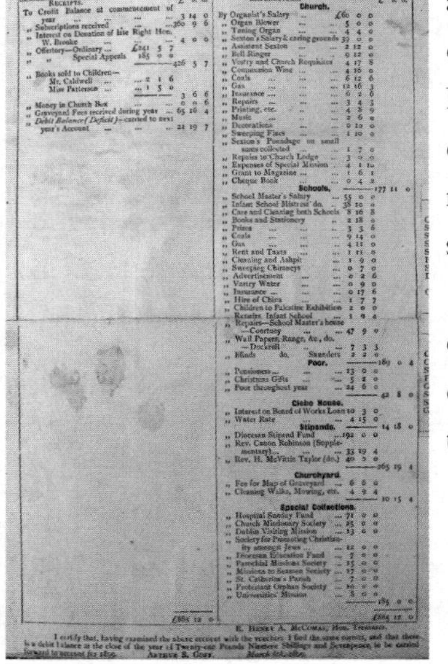

RECEIPTS.		£ s. d.
To Credit Balance at commencement of year ...		3 14 0
" Subscriptions received ...		360 9 6
" Interest on Donation of the Right Hon. W. Brooke ...		4 0 0
" Offertory—Ordinary ...	£241 5 7	
" " Special Appeals	185 0 0	426 5 7
" Books sold to Children— Mr. Caldwell ...	2 1 6	
Miss Patterson ...	1 5 0	3 6 6
" Money in Church Box ...		0 0 6
" Graveyard Fees received during year ...		65 16 4
" *Debit Balance (Deficit)*—carried to next year's Account ...		21 19 7
		£885 12 0

EXPENDITURE.		£ s. d.
Church.		
By Organist's Salary ...	£60 0 0	
" Organ Blower ...	5 0 0	
" Tuning Organ ...	4 4 0	
" Sexton's Salary & caring grounds	39 0 0	
" Assistant Sexton ...	2 12 0	
" Bell Ringer ...	9 12 0	
" Vestry and Church Requisites	4 17 8	
" Communion Wine ...	4 16 0	
" Coals ...	6 12 6	
" Gas ...	12 16 3	
" Insurance ...	6 2 6	
" Repairs ...	3 4 3	
" Printing, etc. ...	4 8 9	
" Music ...	2 6 0	
" Decorations ...	0 10 0	
" Sweeping Flues ...	1 10 0	
" Sexton's Poundage on small sums collected ...	1 7 0	
" Repairs to Church Lodge ...	3 0 0	
" Expenses of Special Mission	4 1 10	
" Grant to Magazine ...	1 6 1	
" Cheque Book ...	0 4 2	177 11 0
Schools.		
" School Master's Salary ...	55 0 0	
" Infant School Mistress do.	38 10 0	
" Care and Cleaning both Schools	8 16 8	
" Books and Stationery ...	2 18 0	
" Prizes ...	3 3 6	
" Coals ...	9 14 0	
" Gas ...	4 11 0	
" Rent and Taxes ...	1 11 0	
" Cleaning and Ashpit ...	1 9 0	
" Sweeping Chimneys ...	0 7 0	
" Advertisement ...	0 2 6	
" Vestry Water ...	0 9 0	
" Insurance ...	0 17 6	
" Hire of China ...	1 7 7	
" Children to Palestine Exhibition	2 0 0	
" Repairs Infant School ...	1 9 4	
" Repairs—School Master's house —Courtney ...	47 9 0	
" Wall Papers, Range, &c., do. —Dockrell ...	7 3 3	
" Blinds do. Saunders	2 2 0	189 0 4
Poor.		
" Pensioners ...	13 0 0	
" Christmas Gifts ...	5 2 0	
" Poor throughout year ...	24 6 0	42 8 0
Glebe House.		
" Interest on Board of Works Loan	10 3 0	
" Water Rate ...	4 15 0	14 18 0
Stipends.		
" Diocesan Stipend Fund ...	192 0 0	
" Rev. Canon Robinson (Supplementary) ...	33 19 4	
" Rev. H. McVittie Taylor (do.)	40 0 0	265 19 4
Churchyard.		
" Fee for Map of Graveyard ...	6 6 0	
" Cleaning Walks, Mowing, etc.	4 9 4	10 15 4
Special Collections.		
" Hospital Sunday Fund ...	71 0 0	
" Church Missionary Society ...	25 0 0	
" Dublin Visiting Mission ...	13 0 0	
" Society for Promoting Christianity amongst Jews ...	12 0 0	
" Diocesan Education Fund ...	7 0 0	
" Parochial Missions Society ...	15 0 0	
" Missions to Seamen Society ...	17 0 0	
" St. Catherine's Parish ...	7 0 0	
" Protestant Orphan Society ...	10 0 0	
" Universities' Mission ...	8 0 0	185 0 0
		£885 12 0

E. HENRY A. McCOMAS, Hon. Treasurer.

I certify that, having examined the above account with the vouchers, I find the same correct, and that there is a debit balance at the close of the year of Twenty-one Pounds Nineteen Shillings and Sevenpence, to be carried forward to account for 1899. ARTHUR S. GOFF. March [illegible]

This book will not describe in detail the administrative and financial changes that took place with disestablishment. Suffice it to say that the

Left and next page: Extracts from Taney Parish accounts of 1898, held by the Representative Church Body library.

Comparative Statement of Funds.

	1894. £ s d.	1895. £ s. d.	1896. £ s. d	1897. £ s. d.	1898. £ s. d.
Offertory	193 1 4	177 14 1	238 2 3	245 4 4	}
Sermon for Stipend fund ...	27 12 4	24 7 6	26 15 7	16 17 6	} 241 5 7
Sermons for Missions & Charities	136 10 10	126 17 4	169 10 0	190 10 0	185 0 0
Stipend Fund	114 7 0	99 15 6	110 18 0	}	
Subscriptions-in-Aid	83 5 0	90 4 0	132 9 0	} 384 4 0	360 9 6
Pew Rents	139 15 6	143 0 6	145 10 6	}	
Sundries	74 9 11	69 2 9	42 16 1	61 13 0	7 7 0
Harvest Thanksgiving Collection for Church Funds	*37 0 0	...	...	...	...
Graveyard Receipts	...	...	47 0 2	52 19 4	65 16 4
Total	806 1 11	731 1 8	913 1 7	951 8 2	859 18 5

Comparative Expenditure.

	1894. £ s. d.	1895. £ s. d.	1896. £ s. d	1897. £ s. d.	1898. £ s. d
Clergy Stipends, balance of ...	100 0 0	100 0 0	69 1 10	75 7 6	73 19 4
Church	161 17 10	167 7 5	198 0 7	273 5 1	177 11 0
Schools	147 15 0	146 1 6	141 1 10	144 10 5	189 0 4
Poor	47 10 4	40 3 4	50 3 0	49 10 5	42 8 0
Glebe	14 18 0	14 18 0	14 18 0	14 18 0	14 18 0
Stipend Fund	191 15 0	192 6 6	192 0 0	192 0 0	192 0 0
Sermons for Missions & Charities	136 10 10	126 17 4	169 10 0	190 10 0	185 0 0
Graveyard Expenditure ...	..	...	32 17 2	12 5 0	10 15 4
Total	800 7 0	787 1 8	867 12 5	952 6 5	885 12 0

* Includes Proceeds of Entertainment.

Constitution drawn up in 1870, and amended frequently since then, provides an excellent basis for the management of the new Church. It gives the laity considerable influence and responsibility (presuming of course a more leisured laity than we have today), and provides a bond between clergy and lay members.

Today in Taney, twelve members are elected by the registered vestrymen to the Select Vestry on an annual basis, at the Easter General Vestry. Any lay person who has attained the age of eighteen years, and who is a resident of the Parish or an accustomed member, may be entered upon the register. Also at the Easter General Vestry, a church warden is nominated by the rector for each church, a second church warden for each church is elected by the registered vestrymen, and two glebe wardens are appointed, by the rector and the vestrymen respectively. The church wardens have responsibility for the administrative aspects of the churches, while the duty of the glebe wardens is to ensure the maintenance of church property. The church wardens and glebe wardens are, like the clergy, ex-officio members of the Select Vestry. Triennially, Taney also elects nine diocesan synodsmen, who, along with the clergy, represent the Parish at the Diocesan Synod, and nine supplemental synodsmen stand in when necessary. Also elected are four parochial nominators, and four supplemental parochial nominators, who take part in the proceedings to appoint a new member of the clergy, should a vacancy arise in the Parish.

The clergy are employed and paid by the Representative Church Body. The Parish is assessed and a financial contribution levied according to its resources, based on the number of contributing parishioners and the nature and amount of the endowments held by the Parish.

In the financial year ending 31 December 2016, the Diocesan Assessment for Taney Parish was €116,245, the Diocesan Obligation €22,045 and the Taney Clergy Pension Fund €3,500. The Parish was served by the rector, Canon Robert Warren, and two curates, Reverend Cathy Hallissey and Reverend Nigel Pierpoint. They are assisted by two lay readers, Ms. Trilly Keatinge and Ms. Fionnuala Drury, as well as, from time to time, Reverend Bernie Daly.

Among the new financial arrangements provided for in the Irish Church Act was compensation for existing clergy, which took the form of annuities or a sum in commutation of the annuity. Most opted for commutation and the payment of the capital sum to the Representative Church Body, which then paid their full stipends. However, no provision was made for the financial future of the Church, and re-organisation had to take place, involving the raising of voluntary subscriptions, the setting up of a sustentation fund in each parish, and prudent investment. The provision of Parish expenses had, as illustrated earlier in this chapter, been increasingly met by voluntary effort during the preceding decades, so that parishioners were to some extent accustomed to bearing the financial burden when charges came. They responded generously to the new situation, and so the material as well as the spiritual future of the new Irish Church was ensured.

During the past 150 years, the processes used by Taney Parish to manage and record its income and expenditure have become increasingly efficient. Initially, a 'collector's book' was kept, recording subscriptions in an erratic and untidy fashion. That for the period

December 1889 to February 1919 begins with a note from the Reverend Alfred Hamilton as follows:

> *The Select Vestry earnestly requests those parishioners who do not subscribe regularly to the Parochial Funds to contribute to the support of the church and calls attention to the resolution of the General Synod states 'that it is the duty of every member of the church to contribute to the support of the Parish in which he resides or holds property'.*
>
> *Each subscriber is requested to write his or her name and subscription in this book, to obtain a printed receipt from the collector and to see that the subscription is duly acknowledged in the yearly report.*
>
> *Signed at the request of the Vestry,*
> *Alfred Hamilton D.D.*

Taney Parish had, for some years, been taking regular collections at Sunday services and efforts were made to increase these. The amounts were recorded in the Preachers' Books, which were, and still are, used to record the name of the preacher at each service. The first services of 1 January 1871, at which the preachers were Reverend Alfred Hamilton and Reverend E.A. Carroll, raised a total of £4-3-0d, all of which was handed over to the Sustentation Fund. The monthly total for church collections in that year ranged from £11-15-0d in February to £27-6-8d in December (which included £12-13-7d given on Christmas Day). Later Preachers' Books give more detailed information about offerings for parochial purposes and special collections taken.

Special offertories in 1896 included the following:

Poor Parish Fund	£10-0-0d
Diocesan Religious Education	£15-0-0d
Society for the Propagation of the Gospel	£14-0-0d & £21-0-0d
Clergy Sons' Society	£9-0-0d

Protestant Orphans' Refuge	£8-0-0d
Cottage Home, Dundrum	£6-0-0d
Colonial & Continental Church Society	£5-16-0d
Kildare Cathedral	£6-0-0d
Hospital Sundries	
(£10 of this was given by Lord Pembroke)	£75-0-0d

In addition, over the years, specific collections were made towards the maintenance of church property – the organ and so on. Indeed, these have provided a constant drain on resources to this day. While details differ between then and now, as society has become more sophisticated, the basic patterns remain the same. Money is spent regularly on fulfilling the requirements of the diocesan assessment, on remunerating the organist and Parish staff, on insurance, on repairs and running costs to church property, and on donations to charities. Income is raised by means of direct subscriptions, church offertories (and, since 1942, the Christian Stewardship Scheme, often referred to as the 'Envelope Scheme'), special collections, bequests and the interest thereon, graveyard fees and as a result of fund-raising social events.

Fundraising offers not only an opportunity for socialising and fun and a means of community cohesion, but can also contribute a significant sum of money to the Parish in general and for specific purposes. The Christmas Bazaar brings in a consistent amount each winter, while the Summer Fête, though to some extent weather-dependent, remains the Parish's largest fundraiser. From time to time, social evenings, murder mystery nights, Parish meals, flower festivals, concerts and so on make important contributions.

To take a few typical years, in 1925, net receipts from the Summer Fête amounted to £108-19-7d, while the 1926 Fête report tells us that the cigarette stall raised £14-7-6d, the rifle range £3-12-0d and the nail driving stall £1-4-4d! In 1994, the Fundraising Committee raised £42,000. Of this, the Christmas Bazaar, or Missionary Sale as it was known at that time, contributed £6,000 and the fête grossed over £9,000, despite what the rector described as 'an absolutely horrendous Saturday', while the balance was raised by a variety of other fundraising social events. These days, many local companies, as well as individuals, sponsor and donate to the fête, which typically can earn €20,000 in a good year.

The figures for expenditure naturally grow with inflation too. The accounts for 1985 show the rector's salary as £7,735, pension contributions of £905, PRSI contributions of £400, motoring expenses of £3,378 and a secretarial allowance of £430. The curate's salary was £5,460, and other expenses correspondingly lower than the rector's, the sexton was paid £600, the organists for the two churches received £1,730 and £435 respectively, the part time secretary £750 and the cleaners £1,600.

As can be seen from the accounts for the year 2016 shown overleaf, today's figures are quite different. Running a parish as large as Taney in 2018 requires a huge administrative input. As late as the middle of the 1980s, one part-time Parish secretary was sufficient for the Parish's needs, and this role was ably fulfilled by Audrey Harrison, who retired in May 2014 and sadly died on 5 September 2016.

Taney Parish

Statement of Parish Receipts (excluding Parish Centre)

	2016 **€**	**2015** **€**
Parish receipts		
Direct giving:		
Direct subscriptions	78,786	77,504
Envelope scheme	63,874	71,198
Church collections	17,919	19,739
	160,579	168,441
Tax refund	53,010	60,740
Special collections	21,806	22,349
Harvest appeal	9,745	7,195
Weddings, funerals and baptism donations	1,826	4,160
	246,966	262,885

Fundraising receipts		
Parish Fête	17,224	19,314
Concerts		380
Christmas Bazaar	8,603	7,498
Lenten lunches	2,505	2,000
Synod	____	617
	28,332	29,809
Other receipts		
Rental of Parish property	29,637	27,974
Sundry	4,262	5,523
Church review and church gazette	3,357	3,000
Photocopying and outside service sheets	729	854
	37,985	37,351
Total Parish receipts	**313,283**	**330,045**

Taney Parish
Statement of Parish Receipts (excluding Parish Centre) (Continued)

	2016 **€**	**2015** **€**
Parish Payments:		
Stipends and remunerations:		
Diocesan assessment	116,245	98,044
Diocesan obligation	22,045	22,335
Organist	16,298	16,824
Resident and visiting clergy stipends	200	1,700
Taney clergy pension fund	3,500	2,500
	158,288	141,403
Establishment Expenses:		
Insurance	13,499	13,485
Repairs and maintenance	19,536	13,656
St. Nahi's grounds keeping	9,669	7,326
Electricity	11,838	5,177
Church oil costs	2,385	4,388
Residential property tax	1,719	1,719
Telephone	629	612
Fire and security alarms	565	960
Waste charges	349	326
Residential water charges	____	188
	60,189	50,461

Administration:		
Parish office salaries	24,477	18,427
Stationery, postage and photocopying	6,102	13,499
Other costs	8,854	7,944
Church review and church gazette	3,456	3,706
Bank interest and charges	1,989	2,050
Computer and website costs	5,027	3,717
Printing	1,682	1,666
Audit fees	1,440	1,200
	53,027	52,209
Missions and charities per Note 4	38,353	40,312
Total Parish Payments	**309,857**	**284,385**

Taney Parish

Statement of Parish Centre Receipts & Payments

	2016 **€**	**2015** **€**
Parish Centre receipts		
Rental of Parish Centre – non-Parish activities	115,186	109,274
Rental of Parish Centre – Parish activities	20,895	17,739
Coffee shop	(666)	215
	135,415	127,228
Parish Centre payments:		
Salaries	64,300	62,979
Repairs	13,394	13,812
Electricity	14,374	16,135
Gas	8,081	8,937
Water rates	788	3,380
Insurance	4,260	4,260
Staff training costs	1,115	
Cleaning supplies	3,148	4,082
Waste charges	2,206	1,425
Fires and security alarms	4,702	2,686
Telephone	530	1,293
Brochure	763	946
	117,661	119,935
Parish Centre net receipts	**17,754**	**7,293**

Taney Parish
Statement of Missions and Charities Payments

Note 4	2016 €	2015 €
Parish Centre receipts		
Alice Leahy Trust	500	
Alzheimer's Society	300	750
ARC cancer support	500	
Armenian Church		500
Archbishop's Training for Ministry Fund	650	1,368
Bishop's Appeal	3,566	4,000
Bishop's Appeal Nepal collection		2,500
Blackrock Hospice in memory of Charlie Nangle	491	
Bóthar	500	500
Cancer Clinical Research Trust		1,716
Christian Aid	2,936	2,790
Church Ministry for Healing	250	250
CMS and missionary outreach	1,500	1,500
CMS – Deirdre Lloyd	1,000	1,000
Country Air	500	500
Diocesan Board of Education	350	350
Diocese of Dublin organ training	750	750
Dublin Simon Community	500	
Focus Ireland		500
Habitat for Humanity		250
In-service training	440	650
Irish branch Royal British Legion in memory of Dick Cooke	250	
Irish Cancer Society		1,000
Irish Hospice Foundation		500
Laura Lynn (Songs of Praise)	400	
Leprosy Mission	350	300
Living Well with Dementia in memory of Rodney Cochrane	764	
Médicines san Frontières	1,000	
Merchant's Quay Ireland	500	
Our Lady's Hospice in memory of Eric Bryan	453	
P.A.C.T.	300	250
Parish Needs Special Trust	10,000	10,000

Peter McVerry Trust	1,000	1,000
Pieta House	500	500
Protestant Aid	3,000	3,000
Protestant Orphan Society	1,000	1,000
The Royal British Legion – Poppy Appeal	751	838
The Royal Hospital in memory of Audrey Harrison	1,361	
The Samaritans	300	300
South American Missionary Society	300	250
Taney Care Group	166	
Taney mission outreach	750	1,000
United Society (formerly USPG)	300	500
Veteran Support Group in memory of Dick Cooke	250	
	38,353	40,312

As the volume of Parish activities grew with the success of the Parish Centre, it became necessary to employ a second office worker, and Tara O'Rourke joined the staff. As her experience grew, so did the complexities of the job, and she became the Senior Parish Administrator, with enhanced responsibilities including the letting of rooms, oversight of staff and day-to-day running of the Parish Centre. Tara's skills ensure that the centre is used to the maximum, generating income that more than covers its cost. In 2014, Maeve O'Kelly joined the staff as Assistant Administrator. Unfortunately, Maeve moved to another post in 2017, but Tara continues to run the busy office with efficiency, helpfulness and humour.

The Parish employs three people part-time to carry out maintenance and physical tasks, and they are augmented by some knowledgeable and dedicated volunteers and advised by the glebe wardens and the Select Vestry. Outside contractors are engaged for major or complex jobs.

The social life of the Parish is greatly enhanced by the presence of the coffee shop, situated in the foyer of the Parish Centre. This is owned by the Parish, but is privately run and staffed from Monday to Friday during office hours. It is also used by parishioners at other times.

In modern times, Taney Parish is a large enterprise, centred on worship but with an extensive administrative and financial structure. This ensures that the Parish runs smoothly and viably, and that the careful planning, budgeting and account-keeping by members of the Select Vestry, the financial sub-committee, the Honorary Treasurer, the Parish Registrar, the auditors and others are responsibly carried out.

The very capable Parish Administrator, Tara O'Rourke, at work in the parish office.

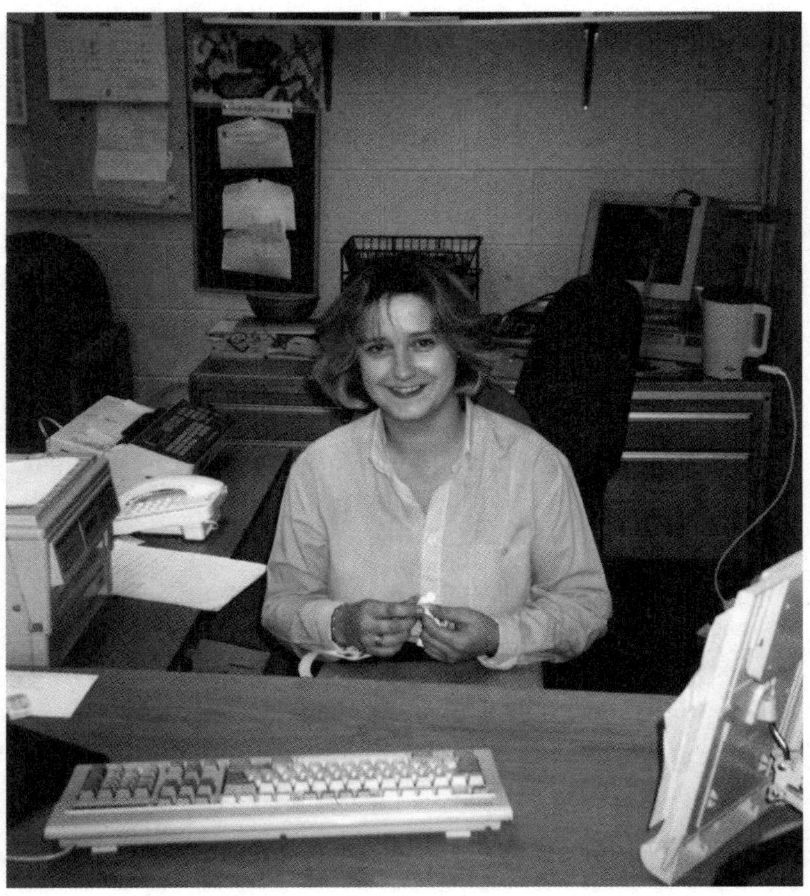

CHAPTER 12

TANEY PARISH PRIMARY SCHOOL

Taney Parish Primary School is the largest Church of Ireland primary school in the Republic of Ireland, with around 450 pupils and twenty-three teachers at present, as well as a number of ancillary employees. This means that class sizes, at under thirty pupils per class, are significantly smaller than twenty-five years ago, enhancing the learning experience of each child.

The staff consists of the Principal, sixteen class teachers and six resource/learning support teachers, as well as the school Secretary, five special needs assistants, two classroom assistants, a caretaker and a housekeeper. For each class grade, from Junior Infants to Sixth Class, there are two classes.

The Principal's role is to manage the school on a day-to-day basis on behalf of the Board of Management. When one visits, it is evident that this task is currently being carried out very successfully, with a happy, caring and friendly staff and children.

Taney Parish Primary School is a co-educational primary school within the state system. It operates under the ethos of the Church of Ireland, and the moral values of that Church permeate school life. There is a close connection with Taney Parish, whose clergy take weekly assemblies. At Christmas, Easter and on other special occasions, the children attend school services in Christ Church Taney.

The admissions policy does, however, admit children of other denominations and faiths or of none, when places are available, and the atmosphere is one of inclusivity of all. As it is over-subscribed, unfortunately not everyone who would like to can obtain a place.

The primary school curriculum taught in Taney is a full one, and fulfilling every child's academic needs is regarded as very important. The current curriculum comprises Irish, English, Maths, Science, History and Geography (the last three of these coming together under the umbrella of Social, Environmental and Scientific Education), Music, Social, Personal and Health Education, Physical Education, Drama, Art and Craft, and Religious Education. After-school activities include sports, mainly hockey and soccer but also cricket, swimming, Gaelic football and tag rugby, as well as French and Spanish language classes. The school is also fully computerised. Musical instruments are taught, specifically recorder, piano and violin, and there is a school orchestra. There is a modest fee for these extra subjects.

All of this is a very long way from the school's origins in the nineteenth century. While we do not know the exact date of the inauguration of the Parish school, evidence of a school at Taney appears in the very earliest Parish record now available to us, the Vestry minutes book of 1791, which indicates the existence of a school, provided for by parochial funds and charitable subscriptions, as early as 1790. Here we find accounts for the years 1790–92 for 'The Charity School of Tanee Parish'. We note, for example, that an annual charity sermon, given in August or September, raised £23-6-4d, £46-12-9d and £62-16-0d respectively in each of these years, while donations received included 11/4½d from the curate, Reverend W. Campbell; £4-11-0d from Lord Trimbleston in 1791; and £2-5-6d from Lord Fitzgibbon in 1792. Some of this was used to pay the schoolmaster £4-11-0d on 31 May 1792, while 'several sums be collected off this parish as usual' for payment that had been authorised to a James Barrett for sand and stone formerly supplied by him for the schoolhouse.

At a meeting of the treasurers, governors and subscribers to the school, held on 4 October 1792, it was revealed that the treasurer held, on behalf of the school, the sum of £100-13-0½d, which excluded a further £7-0-2½d due from the Parish. John Sweetman (a Roman Catholic) and James Potts (a parishioner) were appointed governors, and the following expenditure approved for the ensuing year:

Master	£15-0-0d
Mistress	£6-0-0d
Coals etc	£5-0-0d
Books etc	£2-10-0d
For clothes for any number under 30 boys, sum not exceeding	£22-15-0d
Food	£15-0-0d
Materials for work	£10-0-0d
Sundries	£3-0-0d
	£79-5-0d

The charitable sermon continued to draw funds for the school throughout the subsequent decades, and its frequency was increased to twice per year between 1836 and 1858. The revenue from these, however, was gradually superseded by that from the subscriptions. The school catered for children of all denominations, and it provided food and clothing for pupils where needed. In addition, school funds helped out on a broader parochial level, providing poor families with loans and provisions. The school treasurer thus held quite a pivotal role within the Parish, though a committee was also set up in April 1812 'to manage the said fund to purchase provisions and conduct the distribution thereof ... to meet weekly at the school room every Thursday morning at 10 o'clock'.

The first school master at Taney of whom we have knowledge was Henry Curran, appointed in May 1790 by licence from the Archbishop. One of the earliest schoolmistresses was Mary Brown, who sadly was made redundant due to advancing age. The Vestry meeting of 8 June 1824 had to resolve that 'in consequence of the

Students of Taney Primary School in costume for their production of the drama *Wedding of the Painted Doll*, mid-1930s.

Association for Discountenancing Vice, the present school mistress (Mary Brown) be removed from her situation, being incapable from age of discharging the duties of the situation. Resolved also, that the said Mary Brown be allowed ten pounds per annum by the Parish, in consideration of her having been 13 years the servant of the parish, to be discontinued whenever she is provided with a comfortable asylum, and that the church wardens are hereby authorised to pay her the said sum of ten pounds in two-half-yearly instalments.'

Another teacher who was encouraged to resign was a later mistress of the Infant School, Mrs Caldwell. When the Vestry meeting of 15 April 1901 resolved that the Infant School be amalgamated with the Boys' and Girls' School after the summer holidays of that year, it was decided that Mrs Caldwell 'be informed of the Resolution of the Vestry, with an intimation that if she places her resignation on the board of the Vestry to operate from 1 July next, that the Vestry will give her a retiring allowance of £20 a year for five years or the sum of £60'. Her husband, Edward, had been the principal of the main school from 1862 until it joined the National School System in 1898. On his retirement, Edward Caldwell was presented with an elaborate illuminated address in honour of his service as school master, and this document is carefully retained in Taney School to this day.

The first principal teacher under the National School System was Joseph McCaughey of Strangford, County Down (1898–1928), whose wife Mary also taught in the school until 1938. Mr McCaughey's initial salary was £30 per annum, increased in October 1902 to £48 per annum. He was succeeded by Ernest Costello (1928–46), Thomas Anderson (1946–59) and Robert Smith (1959–78). Mr Smith's wife, Catherine, joined Taney as a teacher in 1961. Mrs Beryl Tilson, who joined Taney as a teacher in 1968, became principal in 1978. Mrs Tilson's leadership brought many benefits to the school in terms of expansion and development. When she retired in 2000, her work was carried on by Mr William Stuart over ten very productive years. Mrs Elizabeth (Lily) Carpenter took over as principal in November 2010. Her role is primarily administrative, managing the school on a day-to-day basis, and, like her recent predecessors, she works tirelessly to run a happy and successful primary school.

During its early decades, the school was run in a house beside the lower edge of the graveyard. An 1869 map of the graveyard, now held by the Representative Church Body, shows its location. It appears, however, that by the 1830s, the Boys' School was housed in part of the old church, while the Girls' School remained in the original house. The separate Infants' School was run in one of the church cottages (now the sexton's home) from the 1820s until it amalgamated with the Boys' and Girls' School in 1901. Indeed, the *Parliamentary Gazetteer* of 1846 describes Taney Parish as a geographical whole as having six daily schools, with a total of 193 boys and 203 girls on their books. The Parish Infants' School was paid for by private donations.

The Boys' and Girls' Parochial Schools were at this time supported by the Charity Sermon, a grant from the London Hibernian Society and £20 a year from the clergyman. Meanwhile, two Roman Catholic free schools had been set up, supported by a charity sermon and a grant from the National Board of Education, while the London Hibernian Society had established a school paid for by a grant from the said Society and private subscriptions.

In 1859, a new parochial school house with school master's residence was built in Eglinton Terrace by Lord Pembroke, who, on 16 November 1878, granted a lease on the building and grounds to the Representative Church Body for 150 years from 25 March 1878 at 1/- a year. The lease contained a covenant by the lessees, that the schoolhouse was to be used only as a parochial school under the Church of Ireland, and for no other purpose without the permission of the lessor. The freehold was finally bought out from Pembroke Estates by the Parish in 1989, so that the schoolhouse and adjoining hall could be sold to provide capital towards the provision of the new Parish Centre.

Taney School joined the National School system on 1 November 1898, following a decision to that effect by the Select Vestry. From then, detailed formal records were kept in the form of school report books, general registers and daily roll books. These provide us with a wealth of information about pupil numbers, the social backgrounds and religious denominations of the children and their eventual destinations on leaving school, as well as interesting administrative detail. The first school report book (1898–1902) tells us that Taney National School's roll number was 15284, and that it was in the townland of Dundrum, the Parish of Taney, the barony of Rathdown, the county of Dublin, and the Poor-Law Union of Rathdown. The garden covered an area of twenty-six perches, thirty-four yards and three feet; the house had a rateable value of £10; the school rooms measured sixty feet in length and twenty-one feet in breadth; there were eight desks and forms, each eight feet in length; and the teacher had free residence.

The first General Register (1898–1938) gave careful instructions as to how it should be kept. Separate registers were to be kept for pupils of each sex. The religious denomination was to be ascertained from the parent (the father, if alive) or guardian of the pupil, and was to be entered as follows: R.C. (Roman Catholic); E.C. (late) (Established Church); Pres. (Presbyterian); Meth. (Methodist). It was the teacher's duty to keep the register neatly and accurately, wholly free from blots and erasures, making the entries with due care, and using none but the best ink. In any case where, because of the negligence or carelessness of the teacher, it became necessary to issue a new register to a school, the cost was to be defrayed by the teacher.

The first roll book, meanwhile, gave equally clear instructions, together with extracts from the Irish Education Act of 1898. The latter prescribed that the parents of children not less than six years old and not more than fourteen were obliged to ensure that their child attended for the required number of days unless there was a reasonable excuse for non-attendance. The requirement was for attendance for seventy-five days in each half-year, but in practice there was a broad range of acceptable excuses for non-attendance. A child over eleven was not required to attend if he or she had received a Certificate of Proficiency in reading, writing and elementary arithmetic. A child who did not have, within two miles of his home by the nearest road, a national school or other efficient school to which the parent of the child did not object on religious grounds, did not have to attend. A child 'prevented from attending school by sickness, domestic necessity, or by reason of being engaged in necessary operations of husbandry and the in-gathering of crops, or giving assistance in the fisheries, or other work requiring to be done at a particular time or season, or other unavoidable or reasonable cause' was excused. Equally so were children under seven who lived too far from a school even though the distance was less than two miles, and those who were in receipt of suitable elementary education elsewhere. School attendance was clearly not accorded quite the priority it is today.

During the first term, twenty-three boys and thirty-five girls were entered on the register between 1 November and 15 December 1898. All of these were members of the Church of Ireland, with the exception of the three Munroe sisters, who were Presbyterian. Their Christian names illustrate the fashion of the time, with Minnie, Bertie, Lily, Ina, Maude, Mina, Lizzie, Henie and Violet among their number.

The first five girls registered were Lily McKnight (aged nine), Jane Sparks (aged ten), Minnie Wilson (aged thirteen), Georgina Durham (aged nine) and Katie Price (aged twelve). The first five boys were Bertie Pierce (aged eight), Robert Wilson (aged eleven), Samuel Blackburn (aged ten), George Carroll (aged eight) and William Tyndall (aged ten). Lily, Jane, Minnie, Bertie, Samuel, George and William had never been to national school before. Georgina had come from Clondalkin Infants, Katie from St Mary's and Robert from St Enoch's in Antrim. Katie was an orphan, while the occupations of the parents of the others were given as a tailor, a laundry foreman, a gardener, a groom, four clerks and a labourer. Lily left at fourteen to go into 'business', Jane at nearly eleven to go to Dublin, Minnie at fifteen, Georgina at thirteen and Katie at nearly fifteen. Bertie left at eleven to go to England, Robert at fifteen was marked 'gone away', Samuel had 'gone away' at twelve, George had 'gone away' at nearly ten, and William left at twelve, destination unknown.

A number of children in the early years were orphans, and little information was recorded about them; they tended to leave Taney before completing their education, frequently at eight or ten years of age, and were often simply marked off the register as 'gone away'. Many orphans left to work in mills and factories at a young age. Lizzie Connell left the school in March 1899 to go into domestic service at thirteen, while Bridget Ennis did so at only eleven years of age.

The old parish hall on Eglington Terrace, which previously housed the parish school.

Sadder still are the records of children who died – for example, two little seven-year-old girls, Alice Johnson and Lizzie Moynes, were to die on the same day, 1 April 1904.

The social backgrounds of the children at Taney Parish Primary School in the earlier part of the century were primarily, though not entirely, working-class. Fathers' occupations tended to be of the skilled manual, semi-skilled and unskilled varieties. They included shopkeepers, butchers, herdsmen, grooms, gardeners, coachmen, carpenters, printers, carters, butlers, railway porters, dairymen and general labourers. During the First World War, several soldiers also featured. There were, however, occasional 'gentlemen', civil servants, engineers and doctors among the parents too. Gradually, the numbers from manual backgrounds were superseded by those from middle-class homes, until, by the 1970s, there had been a huge change in the social complexion of the school, with the vast majority coming from non-manual and professional households. Moreover, while no children in the early years are recorded as

Taney school (**above**) around 1938, and (**below**) around 1940.

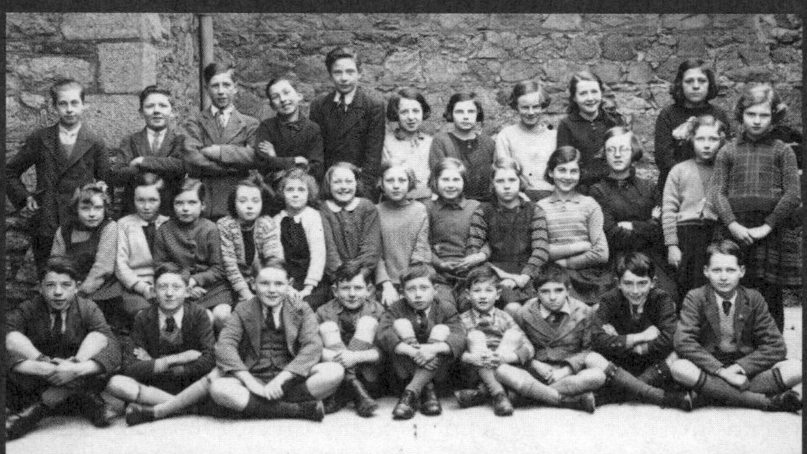

Below: Headmaster Tom Anderson and the Taney pupils, mid-1950s

having gone on to secondary schools, with many entering employment at only twelve to fifteen years of age, by the 1970s, all were, of course, proceeding to secondary schools.

The numbers of pupils on the Taney school roll fluctuated little up to the 1960s, generally averaging an annual total of less than 100. However, demographic changes in Dublin city and county have resulted in a huge growth in the population of Dundrum during the past 500 years. The small rural village developed into a suburban area, as the surrounding farms and estate lands provided a ready supply of relatively low-cost development land, suitable for the building of housing estates. Demand for school places grew, and the old school buildings were no longer adequate

. A two-acre site was found at Sydenham Villas and a new school building, designed by Mr J. Ward and Mr M. Daly of the Office of Public Works, was erected. It was originally planned as a six-teacher school, but an extra classroom was added during construction and, immediately, a prefabricated classroom also became necessary.

The new school was opened by Padraig Faulkner, the then Minister for Education, on Saturday, 21 November 1970. It had cost approximately £45,000, of which the local contribution was to be twenty-five percent. The school was the largest Protestant primary school in the Irish Republic, with 310 pupils on the roll and eight permanent teachers. However, the population of the school continued to grow apace throughout the 1970s, aided in part by the fact that several Protestant secondary schools had moved out from the city centre to the surrounding area. Every two years, more temporary classrooms were added as the school developed, reaching its maximum size in 1979 with a principal, sixteen class teachers, a remedial teacher, two assistants and over 550 pupils.

During the 1970s, the school became more crowded, while half the classrooms were in unsatisfactory, short-term prefabricated buildings. In December 1979, the Board of Management applied to the

Department of Education to have a larger administrative area, a library, a staffroom, staff toilets and a storage room for PE equipment added. The response was positive, but there were no further developments until January 1984, when the Department informed the chairman and principal that the plans had not been approved, as such a piecemeal extension would obstruct any permanent structure which might be built in future to replace the prefabs. The Board of Management then submitted revised plans, which were agreed to in principle by the Department in June 1984. Negotiations continued, and by November 1986, the Department was indicating that a grant of ninety percent of the projected cost of £644,000 would be sanctioned. Further delays occurred, however, and in February 1988, the Board of Management was advised that due to the financial constraints on the Government, the building programme would have to be postponed until early 1989.

Meanwhile, the prefabricated buildings continued to deteriorate, despite voluntary efforts to maintain them. Revised plans were prepared by architect Denis Handy, and were submitted in 1990. These were approved by the Department, and by late 1992, full planning approval had been obtained, an appeal by local residents having been overcome. By Easter 1994, the new building, incorporating eight new classrooms, a special purpose-built remedial room and a new general-purpose room, were complete and in use. The Department of Education sanctioned a grant of £429,547.50, which would provide around eighty-five percent of the funding, with the community contribution covering the remaining fifteen percent plus the cost of the new general-purpose room.

Now the school seemed much more spacious and flexible, but after another ten years, it became apparent that more space was needed for physical education and extra activities. In 2005, the general-purpose hall was extended, a new library and learning-support room and music rooms were added, and the offices of the principal and secretary were extended. In 2009, the old flat roofs were replaced with pitched roofs. Today it feels modern, spacious and comfortable.

The Board of Management of the school at Taney was for many generations chaired by the rector of the Parish, but more recently there has been a lay chairman, currently Dudley Dolan. There is a strong and vibrant Parent–Teacher Association, involved in the organisation and provision of extra-curricular activities, fundraising and other events, and contributing to the smooth relationships in the school.

Taney Parish Primary School has come a long way. It is a large, popular and effective school, which feels happy and caring. As it reaches 120 years as a member of the Irish National School system, it looks forward to a vigorous and successful future.

Mrs Christie's Junior Infants class, tired after Taney Sports Day, 1991.

CHAPTER 13

TANEY VILLAGE – AN UNREALISED AMBITION

An up-to-date history of the Parish would not be complete without a chapter about Taney Sheltered Housing Project, later named Taney Village. I was asked to research and provide this for the Parish.

The development of Taney Village was an innovative and progressive idea. The intention was to build a complex of sheltered housing, in the form of apartments, and a nursing home, close to Taney Road in Dundrum.

An atmosphere of optimism and excitement prevailed in the early years of the twenty-first century, as Ireland experienced unprecedented, albeit ultimately illusory, economic prosperity. At this time, many parishioners wished to see sheltered accommodation developed within the Parish, to give them a sense of security in their older age. The Department of Social Welfare confirmed that the demography of this area was indicative of a need for such facilities now and into the future. The project would meet an established need.

Those members of the Parish who gave a great deal of time, energy and enthusiasm to work towards its realisation did so in the belief that this daring venture was being undertaken in the best interests of the people of the Parish and community. However, the economic collapse of 2008 led to many investors and developers throughout the country losing huge sums. Unfortunately, in spite of the combined efforts of Taney Village Ltd. and the Select Vestry, together with helpful advice from the Diocesan Councils and Glebes and Finance Committees and the RCB Property Committee, the Taney Village scheme did not succeed.

During intensive discussions with several members of the former Taney Village Committee about why the scheme failed, I was informed that it was due to factors outside of the control of Taney. A large amount of research had been carried out into nursing homes and sheltered housing. Every effort was made to get things right. The economic recession beginning in 2008, and the concomitant collapse in property prices, along with inaccurate advice that things should be put on hold as the downturn in the economy would last a maximum of eighteen months, led to the ultimate abandonment of the plan.

Of course, it is inevitable that, over the length of time during which the scheme was planned and discussed, ideas were revised a number of times and delays occurred. This was an enormous undertaking for a parish committee. However, in all respects, the Parish and those parishioners who worked hard and with commitment on this project had the best of intentions. After all, as you will read later in this book, Taney Parish has had a history of providing socially for the people of its community.

Here is a brief account, based on scrutiny of Parish records – and particularly on minutes of the Select Vestry from 1985 to 2013 and those of the Taney Village Committee dating from January 2001 to April 2013, plus available correspondence – as well as discussions with various parties involved in concluding the final negotiations, of what happened.

I have declined to name individuals or companies concerned, in the interests of confidentiality.

* * *

The first suggestion in Parish records of the possibility of the Parish providing facilities for retired parishioners occurred at a meeting of the Select Vestry in May 1985. Discussion took place to consider whether the Building & Finance Committee should buy Altamont Hall on Stoney Road. This would offer the advantages of having all the church property on one site, including a new purpose-built rectory and parish centre, with the possibility of developing other facilities. The meeting concluded that the proposal was exciting but not realistic.

At a subsequent meeting, it was agreed that the Parish's solicitor should be asked to attend the auction for Altamont and bid on behalf of the Parish. In the event, nothing came of this.

At the Easter General Vestry in 1997, the then rector, Canon Desmond Sinnamon, reported that in the previous May and June, the Select Vestry had carried out a Parish survey, the results of which indicated a real interest in the idea of the Parish providing sheltered accommodation. As a result, serious investigation of such a scheme was underway.

The first minutes available to me of a separate 'Sheltered Accommodation Group' date from 1 February 2000, and ten names are listed as members. In mid-2000, the Parish decided to try to buy a house off Victoria Terrace. By 13 December 2000, representatives of the Parish were enquiring about the possible purchase of another house on Taney Road.

The Select Vestry began to follow up in earnest, and between June 2000 and January 2005, representatives of the Parish held discussions on a proposed joint project with six different housing organisations, but no agreement was reached.

Meanwhile, on 1 January 2002, euros replaced Irish pounds as the new currency, and prices were henceforth given in euros.

On 8 August 2002, the Select Vestry made the decision that the Parish would purchase the two above-mentioned houses. The Taney tennis courts lay between these two sites, and the three together would give a total site large enough for the development of a nursing home and sheltered accommodation in the form of apartments.

On 28 January 2003, a letter of sanction was sent from the bank to the Parish representatives for the granting of a loan of €3,400,000 to the Select Vestry of the Parish of Taney, to buy the two sites adjacent to Taney tennis courts.

Subsequently, many discussions took place about the potential composition of the development – how many nursing home beds, sheltered apartments and parking places were required – and plans to reflect these ideas were drawn up and examined.

Various names had been used to describe the project to date. At the 2004 Easter General Vestry, the rector informed parishioners that 'Last Easter we announced that the Parish had acquired a one-acre site beside the Parish Lawn Tennis Club and opposite the new Luas station … "Taney Village" is the working title we have given to a comprehensive scheme.'

The full site had been acquired by early 2005. In May 2005, the Representative Church Body gave approval in principle to the scheme, subject to certain provisos: that the entire land be vested in the RCB, that the Diocesan councils approve the names of those who would be shareholders/trustees, and that the Rector be a shareholder/trustee.

In January 2006, the Taney Village committee reported to the RCB that it had had a strong attendance at an open Powerpoint presentation the previous October, and had received over 100 expressions of interest, indicating a strong level of demand. They now had an estimate of the development costs, which would be financed by a combination of short-term and long-term loan finance, consortium private finance and down payments by future residents.

The proposed site for the Taney Village project.

Five ownership models for residents were under consideration: Interest-free loan to the operator with licence to occupy; lifetime lease; company shareholding (resident buying a share in a limited owner/operator company); outright ownership; and simple tenancy.

The committee believed the following timescales could be achieved:

- Submission for planning permission/complete finance structures – January 2006
- Allow for third-party appeal – July 2006
- Achieve planning permission/tendering process – September 2006
- Construction – January 2007 to June 2008
- Marketing – January 2007 to June 2008
- Completion – September 2008

Had they been able to adhere to this timescale, there is a strong possibility that the project would have been up and running by the time the recession really began to affect borrowing capabilities and potential buyers' house prices.

A document from Dun Laoghaire–Rathdown County Council, dated April 2006, confirms the seeking of planning permission. It was announced at the Easter General Vestry of 2007 that Dun Laoghaire–Rathdown County Council had granted planning approval, that there had been appeals and that a decision was expected on planning my mid-summer. Planning permission was granted by An Bórd Pleanála in September 2007.

At the 8 January 2007 Select Vestry meeting, it was reported that the Parish had spent €895,000 to date on the Taney Village project, excluding property purchase but including the fees of various professionals, plus €169,888 interest on the bank loan, and the bank loan had been increased to €5 million.

Meanwhile, a draft proposal had been drawn up to move the tennis courts to the church grounds. Two full-size courts, and possibly a third court, could be included with careful design.

A meeting of the Taney Village Committee on 5 November 2007 discussed professional advice just received, giving an estimated cost for the plans as they now stood and warning that, even with investors on board for the nursing home together with sales of the apartments, there would be a shortfall of some €5 million.

In May 2008, a new professional and optimistic presentation was made to parishioners. It described the benefits of the development, with its sixty-four-bedroomed nursing home and seventy-two independent living units, and sought to explain the concept of a 'loan licence' and how the scheme would work. It now said that the aim was for occupation of units before February 2010, and it asked for comments.

Meanwhile, the company now called Taney Village Ltd had been legally incorporated. It had four initial directors.

In June 2008, the Taney Village Committee discussed possible prices for purchasers of apartments. It was agreed that a priority should be that all interested potential buyers should be sent a letter updating them and urging them to pay deposits. In November 2008, it was noted that thirty-five refundable deposits had been received.

Costs continued to rise. By the end of 2008, the total bank loan was €5,431,901. Taney Village Ltd had applied for an increase to €6.4 million, and the bank had asked for a Letter of Comfort from the RCB. This increase was mainly to pay professional fees and interest.

Taney Village Ltd had in the meantime approached other banks with a view to borrowing money for development, without success. In 2010, the Taney Village committee commissioned a report on options from another property development and management company, which reported in April. It laid out at length the pros and cons of Taney Village Ltd's continued involvement in the development, and the potential consequences of the choices the Parish had, whether it continued or sold up and cut its losses. It concluded:

It appears to us that the Parish may not be ideally set up to implement the strategy [to continue the development]. The project needs to be driven full-time. This cannot be solely delivered by a part-time committee … this requires management of the project by a suitably qualified and experienced professional who is knowledgeable of both current market input costs and likely returns.

By now, the Taney Village committee records reported that, 'The bank loan now stands at €5,557,518. A due diligence exercise is being carried out with a potential partner in the development of Taney Village.'

In November 2010, the Parish was informed that during the previous few months, the Select Vestry, through the Taney Village committee, had worked to bring resolution to the Taney Village project, taking professional advice. Twelve potential operators/developers had been identified and approached, and one chosen. On 5 October 2010, the Select Vestry had decided to begin a stage of three months' due diligence with this company, a well-established and viable Irish company in nursing care and supported living.

The original bank was prepared to continue to lend money, providing the due diligence report was satisfactory and this company went ahead with its proposal, but unfortunately this did not happen.

A subsequent letter from the bank stated that they were 'anxious that the debt and the title to the lands be transferred into the name of Taney Village Limited, with relevant mortgages executed over all lands'.

The Select Vestry confirmed on 5 April 2011 an earlier decision of 2008, that the lands be transferred into Taney Village Ltd subject to assurances that the debt would be removed from the Parish and that no residual obligations would remain with the Parish. They were getting legal advice on this, but thought it would offer protection to the Parish both corporately and individually. This meant that Taney Parish and parishioners would be relieved of the Taney Village debt. In the event, on further advice, this did not happen.

At the end of September 2011, Canon Desmond Sinnamon retired as rector of Taney. However, it was to be a year before a new rector was appointed, although Reverend Bernadette Daly kindly agreed in January to work as 'Priest-in-Charge' during the vacancy.

On 19 October 2011, the Archdeacon of Dublin sent a letter to the Parochial Nominators of Taney, advising that the Parochial Organisation and Development Committee of the Dioceses of Dublin and Glendalough had decided unanimously not to call a Board of Nomination for Taney until the Parish had 'formally divested itself of all assets and liabilities resulting from the proposed project'. A letter from the Archbishop of Dublin, on 24 October 2011, confirmed this, saying he had no option but to accept the advice of the Parochial Organisation and Development Committee.

Deliberations continued, as did consultations with the bank and the RCB. On 27 November 2011, when no further progress had been made, it was agreed that all depositors should receive their money back as soon as possible, and a letter explaining the current situation was to be sent with the cheques. On the following 5 January, it was confirmed that the remaining depositors had received cheques returning the amount of their original deposit plus interest.

In early 2012, it was agreed that Taney Parish would provide a loan to Taney Village to pay the creditors, the money to be drawn down from the loan facility to pay the Parish once negotiation with the bank was completed. Negotiations were to take place with the creditors, explaining that only limited money was available, and to agree full and final settlement of their debt.

At a Select Vestry meeting of 16 February 2012, chaired by the rural dean, an email was read out, to the effect that the Archbishop undertook to call a Board of Nomination immediately after Easter, subject to the external auditor's report and clarification and the payment of monies owed to creditors.

By the time Canon Robert Warren arrived as Taney's new rector in September 2012, the committee had conceded that the Taney Village dream might not be realised. While the Parish did have working funds, €5.9 million was owed to the bank and the latest fees had not been paid.

In April 2013, the Select Vestry decided to appoint an expert finance sub-committee to negotiate with the bank. Great skill was employed in the negotiations at the highest level within the bank. Eventually, by September, an agreement was reached, involving Taney selling the properties that had been acquired for the project, and paying off the debt to the bank, while retaining the tennis courts.

Estate agents were selected to sell the lands, the property was put on the market at the end of September and it was sold by the end of October 2013. The money was paid by the end of November, and

Taney received the final letter from the bank on 16 December 2013, stating that the bank debt was cleared.

Subcommittee members also met the outstanding creditors. After negotiations, during which the Parish offered a specific amount on condition that settlement occurred within twenty-eight days, each creditor agreed to settle. By the end of 2013, the debts were cleared.

The final figures for the Taney Village project are given in a financial summary for the beginning of the year 2000 to 31 March 2012, prepared by an independent chartered accountancy firm, together with costs for the period from April 2012 to December 2013. According to this summary, the final cost to the Parish from the investment in the Taney Village project was €1,553,203 over the thirteen years.

Sadly, despite the best efforts of those involved, the admirable ambition to provide a nursing home and sheltered housing for older people could not be fulfilled, and the Taney Village idea was over.

CHAPTER 14

A SOCIAL ENTITY

Taney at the Heart of the Community

Mr Low, having laid before the Vestry the plans and proposals for a Parochial Hall to be erected adjoining the Schoolhouse, Resolved: that the Select Vestry approves of the proposal to erect a Parochial Hall, and that the whole matter be referred to the Building Committee with full power to issue a circular to the parishioners asking for funds, and to take all necessary steps to carry out the proposal upon such funds being provided.

Thus read the minutes of the Select Vestry for 8 February 1897, from a meeting chaired by the then incumbent, Canon John Joseph Robinson.

Prior to this, Taney Parish had already developed something of a social life. In 1867, a Choral Union was established, 'with a view to improving the Church Music, and as a means of promoting friendly and social union among parishioners' (Taney Parish Report, year ending 31 December 1867). This met each Thursday at 7pm in the schoolhouse; the annual subscription was 6/- and the entrance fee 2/6d, and by the end of its founding year it had twenty-three members. A parochial library was also held in the schoolhouse. It comprised over 800 volumes, and was open from 12.30pm to 2.30pm each Saturday; it cost 5/- per year to borrow two books at a time, or one could join for half a year for 2/6d, for three months for 1/3d or for one week at 1d, and borrow one book at a time. Sunday school children were entitled to borrow books for 1d per month.

Then there was the Taney Dorcas Association. Its object was to 'enable the local poor of every persuasion to purchase clothing, blankets etc. at a greatly reduced rate, which the subscriptions each year enable the committee to supply them with. The payments are taken by instalments of any sum, however small, which may be convenient – thus bringing them within reach of even the very poorest, as well as encouraging habits of industry and self-respect.' The sales took place on alternate Saturdays in the school (Taney Dorcas Association, Seventh Annual Report, for year ending 1 October, 1867).

By 1897, parochial organisations included the Dundrum Parochial Benefit Society, the Band of Hope, the Mothers' Meetings, the Gleaners' Union, the Girls' Friendly Society, the Society for Female Education in the East, the Mens' Bible Class, the Ladies' Bible Class and the Sunday School Teachers' Meeting. Note that several of the meetings were held on weekday afternoons, reflecting the expectation that women of the Parish would be available at such times.

The parochial hall was paid for by a combination of private subscriptions and fundraising efforts. The final cost was £1,356-12-0d, plus an additional £378 from a Mr John Low for the porch and vestibule. Building commenced in 1897, and was completed in 1898, and the hall was officially opened on Saturday, 28 May of that year. A debt remained of £528, which was finally cleared in 1904, leaving the way open for full enjoyment of the hall and its facilities.

The availability of the parochial hall allowed for an expansion of Parish social life. New societies sprang up, additional classes were offered, and ever-increasing use was made of the new facility. In 1901, the hall housed the Toy Symphony Concert, the School Concert, amateur theatrics, a ping pong tournament, a bazaar and lectures by a Dr Friel and a Professor Steele, the hiring charges from these helping to defer the maintenance costs of the building. 1901 saw the Mothers' Union, and 1902 the Sowers Band, a children's Bible class, the YMCA Bible class and gym classes begun in Taney. A garden fête yielded £75-4-6d towards the parochial hall account, and the Badminton Club had raised the cost of new lighting and a slot meter for the gas stove. In 1903, the Rifle Club started meeting on Tuesdays and Thursdays. In 1905, the Boys Brigade began to meet on Saturday nights (later disbanded in 1954), and in 1906, the Good Templars' Lodge met on Fridays, while a recreation room was opened up each evening at 7pm.

The 'Report of the Select Vestry for the year ended 31 December 1925' lists the following parochial meetings and classes: the Benefit Society, a children's bible class, the Girls' Friendly Society, social quarterly meetings, the Missionary Services League, the Mothers' Union (who then met in the afternoon) and the Girl Guides.

The 1962 Select Vestry Social Report tells of badminton, Brownies, Guides, lawn tennis, the Men's Club, the Mothers' Union, the Rangers, the Scouts, table tennis, Wolf Cubs, the Guild of Youth and the Rovers. The 1964 edition also mentions the Medical Benefit Society and the Dramatic Society.

Other users included the Women's Work Association, the Taney Workingmen's Club and the Orange Lodge (who rented the hall for 12/- per year prior to the First World War), and those running social functions such as *tableaux vivants*, bazaars and dances. Strict rules were laid down for use of the hall – the Select Vestry were careful to declare, on 10 November 1919, that 'no alcoholic liquors be permitted on the premises', and an application for permission to serve claret-cup at a dance on 16 January 1920 was rejected. In the 1930s and 1940s, a Parish Social Club flourished, and in 1950, the Ladies' Chancel Guild was inaugurated. Children's organisations such as Brownies, Cubs, Scouts and the Youth Club flourished. Missionary sales were held, tennis and golf clubs developed, exercise and dance classes were given, and a music society was started. A Parish magazine was issued in 1959, though the second edition did not appear until 1966. Garden fêtes became annual events. Taney Parish as a social entity thrived.

As the twentieth century proceeded, the parochial hall witnessed a tremendous voluntary contribution to Parish and community life, and the associations and groupings of past eras evolved into the open and vibrant Parish organisations of Taney today. By the second half of the century, Taney Parish had outgrown its parochial hall, and it became necessary to replace it with a larger, more modern and more flexible facility. Finally, on Friday, 25 May 1990, parishioners gathered for a celebration and sharing of nostalgia at the 'Last Night of the Hall'.

Discussions had begun in the late 1970s on how to improve Parish accommodation, and by 1980, two clear proposals were being considered – the improvement and extension of the existing hall; and the construction of a new building in the church grounds. Following lengthy discussions on the location of a new Parish Centre, the Vestry Minutes of 20 June 1984 report that 'the feeling of the meeting favoured siting it in the church grounds'. Legal difficulties arose concerning the possession by Pembroke Estates of the freeholds of the church ground and the Eglinton Terrace premises (including the old school building and schoolmaster's house), but the Parish eventually succeeded in purchasing these for the sum of £5,000. Parish organisations had been consulted on their needs and preferences in relation to the new centre, and in March 1987, Mark Duffy was appointed architect for the project.

The Parish Centre was intended to provide a focus for the spiritual and social needs of all age groups within the Parish. The centre was 'launched' at the old parochial hall on 18 May 1989 and a model of the new building was displayed in the porch of the church. An offer by the Church of Ireland Men's Association to invest a substantial amount of money in exchange for the use of certain Parish facilities was accepted, and the building plans were amended accordingly. On 8 November 1989, everyone was delighted when the old hall unexpectedly raised £433,000 at auction.

This sum, together with the £345,000 contributed by the Church of Ireland Men's Association, permitted a revision of the scheme to allow for a snooker room, an enlarged main hall with two badminton courts and a youth den. The balance was raised by the Parish. Planning permission was granted on 20 September 1989, with the condition that a bond or cash to the value of £5,000 be lodged before development commenced to ensure protection of trees on the site and repair of any damage caused during the construction period. Builder Patrick Brock's tender was accepted, and the forty-six-week contract commenced on 19 August 1990. On 11 November 1990, Archbishop Donald Caird dedicated the foundation stone of the new centre.

The building was completed in September 1991. It adjoins the church, allowing easy access between the two, and the design, on three levels, includes a splendid main hall, with its imposing circular stained-glass window taken from the CIMA's Gregg Hall, as well as changing rooms, a minor hall and a lounge, a snooker room, meeting rooms in a variety of sizes, a youth den, two kitchens, storage spaces and the Parish office. The final cost of the centre is estimated at around £1.07 million, of which £100,000 remained outstanding at the end of 1993.

On the afternoon of Thursday, 21 November 1991, following a Service of Thanksgiving in a crowded Christ Church, at which the Archbishop of Dublin, the Most Reverend Dr Donald Caird, gave the address, the Parish Centre was officially opened by Her Excellency, Mary Robinson, President of Ireland. This marked a fantastic accomplishment by the Select Vestry, the Planning Committee, the Building Committee, the Financial Committee and the parishioners in achieving what the Archbishop in his address described as the 'flagship of the diocese', and what is probably the finest parochial centre on this island.

Clockwise from top left: Taney Mothers' Union, around 1942; Taney Lawn Tennis Club 'tea ladies'; Taney Guide Company, around 1942; Taney Mothers' Union; Taney Lawn Tennis Club at home, around 1940; and a youth football team.

Since then, Parish organisations have blossomed in the warm and comfortable surroundings of the new building, supported by the generous voluntary efforts of many parishioners, who give time and energy as leaders and participants. The Taney Drama Society has been revived, new activities have started and old societies have grown.

Activities within the centre now include the following:

Parish youth organisations – Mums & Toddlers, Ladybirds, Beavers, Brownies, Cubs, Guides, Scouts, Youth Club, Youth Choir and Music Society.

Recreation and sports – Badminton Club, Morning Ladies' Badminton, CIMA Badminton, Parish Snooker, CIMA Snooker, Bowling Club and Taney Lawn Tennis Club.

General Parish interest – Bible Study, Taney Friends and Social Club, Chancel Guild, Choir, Children's Choir, Occasional Chorus, Drama Society, Mothers' Union, Taney Change Ringers' Society, Taney Parent–Teacher Association, Taney Rangers and Taney Play School.

Activities for the community – Art, Children's Artzone, Portfolio Preparation, Dancing (including Irish Dancing, Children's Ballet, Dance & Fitness and Ballroom Dancing), Pregnancy Pilates, Baby Massage, Baby Sign Language, Children's Performing Arts, Bridge (three clubs), Rugby Tots, Playball, Volunteer Stroke Team, Exercise for Life, Badminton, Karate, Pilates, Yoga (three groups), Weight Watchers, Gardening, Swedish and Spanish.

The centre is also used for formal and informal meetings, training days, exhibitions and many social occasions, such as Taney Mothers' Union's centenary celebrations in 2001, the Murder Mystery Night in 2010, the Dream Auction fundraiser in 2012, barbeques, art exhibitions, children's holiday camps and plays. Dublin and Glendalough Diocesan Synod has met here on many occasions. In the summer of 2013 alone, fifteen children's summer camps were booked into the Taney Parish Centre. The Parish Centre coffee shop plays a vital role in all of this, offering encouragement to people to linger and get to know each other.

Taney is a busy parish, with all manner of social activities and fundraisers going on.

PARISH OF TANEY

You are invited to the opening of the Exhibition

"Focus on Famine"

An Exhibition of Words and Images
Commemorating the 150th Anniversary of the Great Irish Famine
and focusing on famine in the world today
on Friday, 24th March 1995 at 7.30p.m.
in Taney Parish Centre.

To be opened by the Archbishop of Dublin, Most Rev. Dr. Donald Caird
Guest Speaker: Luke Dodd, Strokestown Famine Museum

R.S.V.P. Taney Parish Office,
Taney Road, Dur m,
Dublin 14. Tel 298 5491.

xhibition Open
Sat 25th, Sun 26th, Mon 27th, March.

TANEY PARISH

MISSIONARY SALE

SATURDAY, 7th DECEMBER, 1985

10.30 a.m. to 3.30 p.m. in The Parochial Hall

★ ★ ★

Santa arriving 11.30 a.m.

TEA • COFFEE • LIGHT LUNCHES

ADMISSION 10p

In aid of The Church Missionary Society for Bishop Tucker College, Uganda

– STALLS –

Cakes .... Mrs. Gallagher - 981683, Mrs. Sheil - 983849
Country Produce/Delicatessen .... Mrs. Brooks - 987513
Men's Stall .... Mr. Kearon - 982194
Mothers' Union .... Mrs. Rothwell & Members - 982803
White Elephant .... Mrs. Kerr - 982343, Mrs. Sinnamon - 984497
Books & Records .... Mrs. Hamilton - 987043, Mrs. Ryan - 983972
Bran Dip .... Mrs. O'Neill - 988907
Sunday School .... Mr. Barry & Teachers - 698602
Ice Cream Bar .... Gillian Gardiner & Youth Club - 981362
Santa's Cave – Gifts 50p
Refreshments .... Mrs. Kirk - 884766
Lunch Bookings .... Mrs. Duffy - 981455

PARISH OF TANEY

The Rector, Churchwardens & Select Vestry request the pleasure of your company at a

Parish Supper

on Tuesday, 29th January, 1985
in 'Blinkers' Leopardstown Road,
Foxrock, Dublin

Please reply to Lady Visitor who will call in the near future

In 1997, a major flower festival called 'The Celtic Twilight at the Harvest Moon' was held from 17 to 20 September. On Sunday, 20 September, a Festival ecumenical service was held, and the Archbishop of Dublin, Most Reverend Dr Walton Empey, presided. That evening, the Parish hosted a concert, 'A Celtic Musical Twilight', featuring Meav Ní Mhaolchatha (of the Irish choral ensemble Anúna) and Taney Parish Choir with David Adams as Musical Director.

Non-Parish activities contribute substantially to the costs of running the Parish Centre, and also bring in people of all faiths and none from the local community, breaking down social barriers and building upon social connections. The Parish Administrator, Tara O'Rourke, ably manages the letting of rooms, so that it is now fully self-sufficient, covering its own running costs from the income it brings in. In 2015, it made a surplus of €7,293, and in 2016, a surplus of €17,754.

Of course, the Parish Centre needs regular refurbishment and upgrading. Every few years, for example, the kitchens need to be upgraded to meet the new standards of the HSE, and improvements are required around the centre from time to time to meet health-and-safety requirements. The Parish has operated according to a safety statement for the last couple of decades, indicating its intentions to meet safety regulations. Regular fire drills are carried out, and representatives of Parish organisations are trained to use fire extinguishers and defibrillators. There must be a person present at all events who is aware of fire drill procedures.

Like all Church of Ireland parishes, Taney is obliged to operate Safeguarding Trust – volunteers need to be ratified from the point of view of Safeguarding Trust to provide a safe and healthy environment for children and vulnerable adults attending Parish activities and for those who work with children within the Parish. A Parish Safeguarding Trust panel offers guidance on the training needs and obligations of all leaders. The panel assesses complaints, and an information and training session prepares those who will be working with children.

Above: Reverend Bernie Daly, writer and broadcaster John Bowman and Carol Robinson Tweed, at the Mothers' Union, 2013.

The Taney Rangers (**above**) on an outing in 2000, and (**below**) heading to Birr Castle around 2001.

President Mary Robinson at the opening the new Parish Centre, 21 November 1991.

Volunteers for all children's and youth activities are subject to vetting by An Garda Síochána before acceptance.

In recent decades, the Parish has become more disability-conscious. Paths around the outside of the Parish buildings have been made safer and easier to walk or propel wheelchairs on, and a stair-lift has been installed in the Parish Centre. This was presented by Mrs Dolly Turner in memory of her husband Tom Turner (1913–98) on 5 April 2009, and a plaque to that effect has been placed in the Parish Centre.

Parking spaces have been allocated for use by those with disabilities, and space made in the church to facilitate wheelchair users. There is also a plaque on the wall of the centre dedicated to the memory of parishioner Derek Jones (1923–2010), in recognition of his gift of a sound system to the Parish. An induction loop was installed in Christ Church Taney in the 1990s, and sound systems with induction loops were fitted in St Nahi's Church and the major and minor halls of the Parish Centre in 2012.

Volunteering has always been an important part of Taney life. For example, before the advent of the Community Service and Fás schemes in the Parish, volunteers worked at clearing the graveyard. In 2001, a group of parishioners came forward and offered their time and knowledge in helping with the maintenance and planting of the grounds around Christ Church Taney, an offer accepted with gratitude. Today, Parish volunteers help with gardening, maintenance and catering, while different groups of parishioners provide and serve refreshments on most Sundays after the main 10.15am service.

Engagement with others is regarded as a vital part of Parish fellowship and outreach. The Parish has twinned with the Omey group of parishes in west Connemara, and visits there have taken place. Friendship and solidarity is offered to, and received from, the Armenian Community in Ireland. This community, under the chairmanship of Dr Paul Manook, has been worshipping in Christ Church Taney and using the Parish Centre on Sundays since 2009. Taney Parish made

Left: A banner celebrating a century of Taney Mothers' Union branch, displayed in Christ Church Taney.
Below: St Nahi's choir and clergy after the choir lunch, September 2001.
Bottom: Some of the regular Wednesday morning congregation enjoy a coffee in the Parish Centre after service.

Above: Taney Brownies troupe, 1995.

Below: Busy Beavers.

Clockwise from top left: Conor being enrolled in the Beavers, 1993; Scouts heading off into the wilderness; Beavers picking up some gardening skills; karaoke at the Youth Club Christmas party; Taney Ladybirds at 'Jack, Jill and the Drainpipe'; and Beavers planting flower bulbs.

a contribution to the Khachkar memorial, placed in the grounds of Christchurch Cathedral and dedicated on 5 December 2015, in memory of those who perished in the Armenian genocide of 1915.

Parishioners travelled to help at an orphanage in Cluj, Romania, and to help victims of the tsunami in Sri Lanka. A visit also took place to the Holy Land, led by the then rector, Reverend Sinnamon, who had contacts there, to gain a better understanding of conditions for the people. Donations are made every year to a selection of approved charities, as they have been for the past century. Below is a list of donations made in 1961, taken from the 1962 Social Report.

Donations – 1961

Parish Poor Fund	£30-0-0
Grangegorman Poor Fund	£32-0-0
Poor Parishes Fund for Grangegorman Parish	£25-0-0
Earl Haig Fund	£35-0-0
Adelaide Hospital	£35-0-0
Rest for the Dying	£20-0-0
Sunday School Society of Ireland	£15-0-0
Protestant Orphan Society	£20-0-0
Church of Ireland Temperance Society	£6-0-0
Church of Ireland Jews Society	£17-0-0
Church Missionary Society	£33-0-0
Mission to Seamen	£15-0-0
Colonial and Continental Church Society	£21-0-0
Christ Church Cathedral	£20-0-0
Mission to Lepers	£20-0-0
Church of Ireland Labour Yard	£6-0-0
Irish Clergy Sons Educational Society	£25-0-0
South American Missionary Society	£15-0-0
Ballymacarrett Mission	£10-0-0
Haven of Refugees	£12-0-0
Hibernian Bible Society	£5-0-0
Dublin University Mission to Chota Nagpur	£10-0-0
Ordinants Fund	£25-0-0
	£452-0-0

All the fun of the fête: the summer fête and the Christmas Bazaar – something for everyone, with hustle and bustle and good humour all round.

In 1994, the Taney 'Focus on Famine' group of parishioners came together to research the Irish Famine and its legacy. The 'Focus on Famine' exhibition was opened on the evening of Friday, 24 March 1995, in the Parish Centre by the Archbishop of Dublin, Most Reverend Dr Donald Caird, to commemorate the 150th anniversary of the Great Famine in Ireland and draw parallels with famines in the modern world. The guest speaker at the opening was Luke Dodd of the Strokestown Famine Museum.

Taney's exhibition featured the original diaries of an Irish landlord, John Hamilton of St Ernan's, Donegal, chronicling the effects of famine on his estate, as well as photographs, archives of the Relief Commission, literature from current relief and development agencies, a range of visual material including a life-sized model of a cottier's cabin constructed by the Scouts, soup of the type given out during the Famine made by the Guides, thirty-two watercolour paintings by Anne Thérese Dillon and a letter from the Irish Minister for Overseas Aid and Development outlining current Irish aid policy. The exhibition ran for four days, and was accompanied by an ecumenical service on the Sunday, a visit from Taney's Northern Ireland link parish – Ballyholme – and a talk by children's writer Maria Conlon-McKenna.

Over one million people died as a direct result of the Great Famine, many emigrated and the population of the island was halved to four million. It resonates deeply with Irish people, who understand how political injustices can lead to such devastating events and have proved sympathetic and generous to those affected by contemporary famines. The heightened awareness of the Irish experience drew around 2,000 people to the exhibition, which was subsequently shown in a range of other locations, such as Dublin Civic Offices, Armagh Heritage Centre, Tuam Cathedral and libraries. It returned to Taney on 4 March 1996 for another four days.

Top: Parishioners on a trip to Romania, helping to build a children's home.

Middle and bottom left: Building wooden houses and planting trees in tsunami-ravaged Sri Lanka.

Bottom right: Taney School pupils on stage at the Centenary Concert.

Engagement with the wider Irish community is also seen as very important. An example of this, and of the mutual benefits that can accrue, came in the 1980s, as the 1983 Criminal Justice Community Service Act came into force, operated by the Probation and Welfare Service of the Department of Justice. Reverend Sinnamon decided to engage with this, and the author of this book set up and ran several projects within the Parish. This involved carefully assessed, non-violent, non-drug-using offenders being offered an alternative to imprisonment – the opportunity to do unpaid work under the supervision of a foreman paid by the Justice Department.

Work done included refurbishment of the floor of St Nahi's Church, painting of the interior of St Nahi's, three years' work in the graveyard, redecorating of the Parish hall and the curate's house and clearing of the back gardens, painting of classrooms in Taney school, repair and painting of school prefabs and tidying of the school grounds. A qualified engineer who was on a Community Service Order drew up the plans for the burial plot for the interment of ashes. The only costs for the Parish were materials, as labour and administration were supplied by the State. Schemes such as this and the Fás projects that followed, paid for by the Department of Social Welfare, demonstrate in a practical way reciprocal benefits that can arise from Taney's active involvement in the wider Dublin community.

With such a lot going on, good communications are vital. The Parish magazine, *Taney News*, is delivered to all Parish households by volunteers, or posted as necessary. Taney went online in 2001, and a weekly update, *Taney News Extra*, is emailed to all who ask for it, with copies left in the church porch for others. Short registration forms are available in the church for newcomers to fill in if they wish to be contacted. Email is the major form of communication used by the Parish office nowadays. The website www.taneyparish.ie gives detailed information on church services, activities, key personnel, the history of the Parish and contact details, and this is redesigned or updated as needed.

Top: At the Famine exhibition, 1995.

Above: Parishioners celebrating.

The pleasant and congenial atmosphere and wide use of the Parish Centre has broken down many imagined barriers between those of different backgrounds in the Dundrum district, and brought people together in a happy and productive way. Annual events such as the Christmas Bazaar and the Summer Fête also attract many Dundrum residents and show that Taney is now a fully integrated part of the Dundrum community.

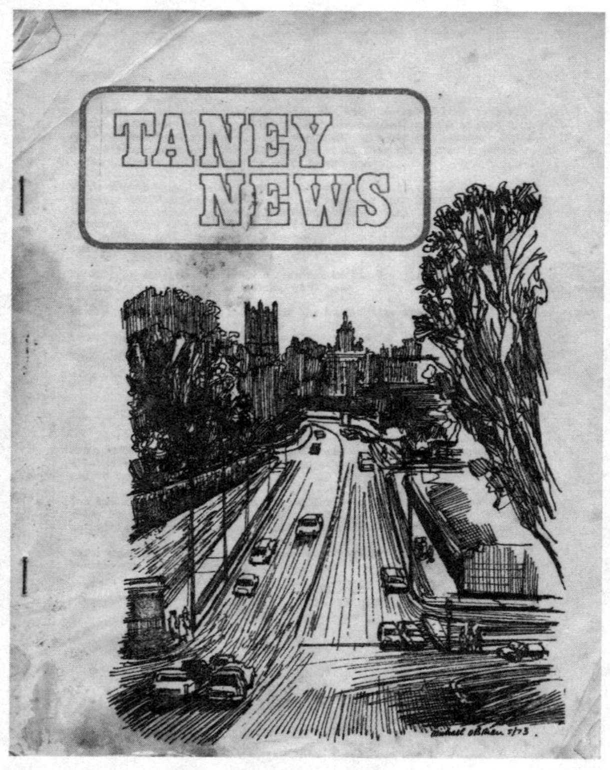

An issue of *Taney News* dating from summer 1973.

CHAPTER 15

TANEY TODAY AND TOMORROW

Plans for the bi-centenary of the opening of Christ Church Taney began to be considered back in October 2015. Suggested physical preparations included full repair and redecoration of the church and improved lighting in the chancel and sanctuary. All these tasks were carried out in the summer of 2017, as was the replacement of the choir pews with good quality choir chairs to allow flexibility of use for services and concerts, the installation of safety glass on the balconies and the removal of some pews at the front of the church to give more space for different activities. The electric wiring has also been upgraded. In addition, a new screen was suspended behind the chancel arch and a projector installed, and new pew cushions have recently been purchased.

A committee was formed to prepare for the realisation in 2018 of some of these ideas. At the time of writing, plans are in train for a concert to be given by the No.1 Army Band on Friday, 27 April, and a bi-centenary festival service will be held on Sunday, 24 June, with Bishop Michael Burrows preaching. A Taney Golf Classic is planned for September, and there will be a flower festival and an art exhibition with the theme 'Reflections of Harvest in Dundrum' during the weekend of 4 to 7 October. An Advent 'Songs of Praise' will also take place with the Stedfast Brass Band on Advent Sunday, 2 December.

While the national trend is that church-going is no longer the priority for some that it once was, and young people's sporting activities on a Sunday morning militate against regular weekly attendance, more families and individuals are joining Taney parish than leaving, and both membership and congregation numbers remain healthy.

Taney Parish Centre, now open for twenty-seven years, continues to bring together parishioners and friends from Dundrum and its environs, for fun, learning and social nourishment. The Centre's position as a social hub helps provide a connection between the spiritual and the social. The links between the church and the primary school are being strengthened. Taney's youth organisations are all doing well. The parish is now once again in a healthy financial position, with strong cash balances. All this augurs well for a dynamic future for an already lively and successful parish.

The energetic endeavours of the Taney clergy, Robert, Cathy and Nigel, help to create a spirit of inclusion, openness and caring, a sense of belonging and trust, which encourages positive engagement with the Parish.

In such a setting, the nurturing of our spiritual life flourishes. The Parish of Taney has come a long way in the past 200 years, and the future looks bright and full of promise.

I hope you have enjoyed this update to my 1994 publication, Taney: Portrait of a Parish. I hope that your interest in Taney, the largest Church of Ireland parish in the Republic of Ireland, has been enriched by an insight into its development, into the historical and social processes which have brought it to its present point. I have attempted, in a balanced and fair way, to satisfy any curiosity readers may have about events that have taken place and issues which have arisen within the parish during the past quarter of a century. An enhanced understanding of what has gone before can only be of benefit in planning for what is to come.

Carol Robinson Tweed

2018

BIBLIOGRAPHY

Primary Sources

Taney Parish Select Vestry minute books:	1791–1813 1813–30 1830–46 1847–60 1861–84 1885–1906 1907–30 1930–58 1958–77 1977–82 (unbound) 1982–93 (unbound) 1993–2017 (unbound)
Taney Parish reports	1865–90 1891–1901 1891–1906 1902–14
Taney Select Vestry Social Report	1962 1964
Annual Report of the Select Vestry for	1923 1925 1961 1963
Taney Parish registers of vestrymen	1870–81 1882–1923 1924–36 1952–84 1984–92 1992–2017
Collector's Book, Parish of Taney	1889–1918
Taney Parochial Fund Book	1889–1914
Taney Parish Registry Book	1814–35 1835–67

Taney Combined Register (1) Baptisms Marriages Burials	 1791–1835 1795–1835 1814–35
Taney Combined Register (2) Baptisms Marriages Burials	 1835–67 1835–59 1835–57
Taney Parish Register of Baptisms	1867–1921 1922–67 1967–2005 2005–17
Taney Parish Register of Marriages	1875–90 1890–1908 1908–31 1931–49 1949–56 1957–71 1971–85 1985–90 1993–98 2002–07 2007–16
Taney Parish Register of Burials	1857–66 1866–83 1883–95 1895–1909 1909–23 1923–50 1950–83 1984–93 1993–2016
Index to burials	1897–1983
Taney Parish preachers' books: old church (St Nahi's)	1907–16 1916–33 1933–51 1984–94

Taney Parish preachers' books: Christ Church	1850–76 1896–1901 1901–07 1907–18 1919–35 1935–47 1947–56 1956–59 1959–65 1965–71 1971–77 1977–83 1984–92 1992–94 2003–15
Taney Social Club registers	1939–40 1944–45
Taney Medical and Benefit Society account books	1952–65 1965–90
Memorandum of Church property 28 October	1887
Graveyard: Plan Graveyard: Alphabetical index to plan Graveyard: Updated list of graves	
Taney branch, Gleaner's Union, misc. papers	1908–14
Reports of Taney parochial schools	(year ending) 31/12/1959 31/12/1860 31/12/1861 31/12/1862 31/12/1863 31/12/1867 31/12/1868 31/12/1869
Taney school report books	1893–1973
Taney school roll books	1898–1986
Taney school general registers	1898–1972
Address to Edward Albert Caldwell	1 November 1898

Lease documents re: Lease by Earl of Pembroke and Montgomery to Representative Church Body:

School Houses – 16 November 1878.

Land attached to Church at Taney – 16 November 1878.

Boards of Management of National Schools – *Constitution of Boards and Rules of Procedure* – Public Stationery Office, Dublin.

Constitution of the Church of Ireland 1989, updated by Statute of the General Synod

Documents contained in the boxes of diocesan records for Taney Parish – Representative Church Body library.

Miscellaneous Loose Papers, 1874–1983, held by RCB library.

Miscellaneous Loose Papers, 1983–2017, held by Taney Parish.

All minutes, notes, correspondence, plans, etc., in the possession of Taney Parish relating to Taney Village 2000–13.

Minutes, Accounts and Correspondence of the Taney Village Committee, 2000–13.

Final Accounts of Taney Village Project, 2013.

Service sheet, 14 September 2001.

Drawings by Michael Judd for the Burrows memorial window, 1994.

Art-Historical Assessment Report No. 11/0000 of the United Diocese of Dublin & Glendalough (2000).

Secondary Sources

Ball, Francis Elrington, and Hamiilton, Everard, *The Parish of Taney: A History of Dundrum, near Dublin, and its Neighbourhood* (Dublin, 1895).

Ball, Francis Elrington, *History of the County of Dublin, Part 2* (Dublin, 1903).

Bowe, Nicola, Caron, David & Wynne, Michael, *Gazeteer of Irish Stained Glass – The Works of Harry Clarke and the Artists of An Túr Gloinne (The Tower of Glass) – 1903–1963* (Dublin, 1988).

Bowen, Kurt, *Protestants in a Catholic State: Ireland's Privileged Minority* (Dublin, 1983).

Butler, Alban, *Lives of the Saints, Vols 3 and 4* (Kent, 1956) (originally published in 1759).

Corlett, Christiaan (ed.), *Unearthing the Archeology of Dun Laoghaire–Rathdown* (Dublin, 2013), Articles by Christiaan Corlett & Edmond O'Donovan.

Eames, Rev. R.H.A., *The Quiet Revolution: The Disestablishment of the Church of Ireland* (Dublin, 1970).

Hurley, Michael S.J. (ed.), *Irish Anglicanism 1869–1969: Essays on the role of Anglicanism in Irish Life* (Dublin, 1970).

Igoe, Vivien, *Dublin Burial Grounds and Graveyards* (Dublin, 2001).

Joyce, Weston St John, *The Neighbourhood of Dublin* (Waterford, 1921).

Leslie, Canon J.B., *Biographical Succession List of the Clergy of the Dublin Diocese, Vol 2* (Dublin, MS 61/2/4/2).

Leslie, Canon J.B., revised, edited and updated by Wallace, W.J.R., *Clergy of Dublin and Glendalough Biographical Succession Lists*, Bound Edition (Dublin, 2001).

Lewis, Samuel, *Topographical Dictionary of Ireland, in 2 Vols* (London, 1837).

McDowell, R.B., *The Church of Ireland, 1869–1969* (Studies in Irish History Series) (London, 1975).

Milne, Kenneth, *The Church of Ireland: A History* (Dublin, 1966).

Parliamentary Gazeteer of Ireland, Vols 2 and 3 (Dublin, 1846).

Shearman, Hugh, *How the Church of Ireland was Disestablished* (Dublin, 1970).

Wilson, Canon W.G., *The Church of Ireland after 1970: Advance or Retreat?* (Dublin, 1968).

Newspaper and Journal Articles

Irish Times, 20 June 1861.

Irish Times, 11 June 1872.

Irish Times, 23 November 1970.

Journal of the Royal Society of Antiquaries of Ireland, Vol. 132 (2002).

Taney News, various issues, 1995–2017.

obrien.ie